SEXUAL HARASSMENT

Other books in the Current Controversies Series:

SEXUAL HARASSMENT

David L. Bender, *Publisher*
Bruno Leone, *Executive Editor*

Bonnie Szumski, *Managing Editor*
Carol Wekesser, *Senior Editor*

Karin L. Swisher, *Book Editor*
Christina Pierce, *Assistant Editor*

CURRENT CONTROVERSIES

Cover photo: SIPA Press/N. Berman

Library of Congress Cataloging-in-Publication Data

Sexual harassment / Carol Wekesser, book editor, Karin L. Swisher,
  book editor, Christina Pierce, assistant editor.
    p. cm. — (Current controversies)
  Includes bibliographical references and index.
  ISBN 1-56510-021-2 (lib. : acid-free paper) — ISBN 1-56510-020-4
  (pbk. : acid-free paper)
    1. Sexual harassment of women—United States. 2. Sexual harassment
  of women—Laws and legislation—United States.   I. Wekesser, Carol,
  1963-   II. Swisher, Karin, 1966-   .   III. Pierce, Christina.
  IV. Series
  HD6060.3.S47   1992
  331.4'133—dc20   92-23593
                                                                   CIP

Contents

Chapter 1: Is Sexual Harassment a Serious Problem?

> In October 1991, law professor Anita Hill charged U.S. Supreme Court nominee Clarence Thomas with sexual harassment. The ensuing testimony spurred debate throughout America concerning the extent of sexual harassment. While many believe that it is a serious problem, many others are confused about what constitutes harassment and are uncertain of how many people are affected by it.

Sexual Harassment Is a Serious Problem

> Sexual harassment is a pervasive problem that too often is unreported or ignored by employers and the government. Because it oppresses women and prevents them from fulfilling their potential, sexual harassment must be stopped.

> Sexual harassment on university campuses is a much more widespread problem than most Americans realize. Universities often protect professors guilty of harassment and do little to help student victims.

> While America's top financial firms are making attempts to decrease sexual harassment, it remains a serious problem. The industry has long been reluctant to accept women fully, and harassment often accompanies this lack of acceptance.

> Although it has instituted sexual harassment policies, the U.S. Navy still has a severe sexual harassment problem. Because the navy is dominated by men, many women find it difficult to report incidents of harassment and to have perpetrators punished.

Chapter 2: What Causes Sexual Harassment?

Many sexual harassment cases have been decided in the courts. The decisions in these cases were contradictory, and many even blamed the women involved for causing the harassment. These unfair decisions have led to even more harassment.

Chapter 3: How Can Sexual Harassment Be Reduced?

Chapter 4: Can Broad Legal Definitions of Sexual Harassment Be Effectively Used in the Courts?

While many people understand exactly how courts define sexual harassment, many others find the definitions confusing.

Broad Legal Definitions of Sexual Harassment Are Effective

Broad Legal Definitions of Sexual Harassment Are Harmful

Foreword

By definition, controversies are "discussions of questions in which opposing opinions clash" (Webster's Twentieth Century Dictionary Unabridged). Few would deny that controversies are a pervasive part of the human condition and exist on virtually every level of human enterprise. Controversies transpire between individuals and among groups, within nations and between nations. Controversies supply the grist necessary for progress by providing challenges and challengers to the status quo. They also create atmospheres where strife and warfare can flourish. A world without controversies would be a peaceful world; but it also would be, by and large, static and prosaic.

The Series' Purpose

The purpose of the Current Controversies series is to explore many of the social, political, and economic controversies dominating the national and international scenes today. Titles selected for inclusion in the series are highly focused and specific. For example, from the larger category of criminal justice, Current Controversies deals with specific topics such as police brutality, gun control, white collar crime, and others. The debates in Current Controversies also are presented in a useful, timeless fashion. Articles and book excerpts included in each title are selected if they contribute valuable, long-range ideas to the overall debate. And wherever possible, current information is enhanced with historical documents and other relevant materials. Thus, while individual titles are current in focus, every effort is made to ensure that they will not become quickly outdated. Books in the Current Controversies series will remain important resources for librarians, teachers, and students for many years.

In addition to keeping the titles focused and specific, great care is taken in the editorial format of each book in the series. Book introductions and chapter prefaces are offered to provide background material for readers. Chapters are organized around several key questions that are answered with diverse opinions representing all points on the political spectrum. Materials in each chapter include opinions in which authors clearly disagree as well as alternative opinions in which authors may agree on a broader issue but disagree on the possible solutions. In this way, the content of each volume in Current Controversies mirrors the mosaic of opinions encountered in society. Readers will quickly realize that there are many viable answers to these complex issues. By questioning each author's conclusions, students and casual readers can begin to develop the critical thinking skills so important to evaluating opinionated material.

Current Controversies is also ideal for controlled research. Each anthology in the series is composed of primary sources taken from a wide gamut of informational categories including periodicals, newspapers, books, United States and foreign government documents, and the publications of private and public organizations. Readers will find factual support for reports, debates, and research papers covering all areas of important issues. In addition, an annotated table of contents, an index, a book and periodical bibliography, and a list of organizations to contact are included in each book to expedite further research.

Perhaps more than ever before in history, people are confronted with diverse and contradictory information. During the Persian Gulf War, for example, the public was not only treated to minute-to-minute coverage of the war, it was also inundated with critiques of the coverage and countless analyses of the factors motivating U.S. involvement. Being able to sort through the plethora of opinions accompanying today's major issues, and to draw one's own conclusions, can be a complicated and frustrating struggle. It is the editors' hope that Current Controversies will help readers with this struggle.

> *"Whether it was unjustified sensationalism or serious journalism, the Hill/Thomas hearings brought the issue of sexual harassment to the forefront of public debate."*

Introduction

In October 1991, Senate hearings involving U.S. Supreme Court nominee Judge Clarence Thomas and law professor Anita Hill dramatically focused the nation's attention on sexual harassment. During these hearings, Hill testified that Thomas had sexually harassed her ten years before while they worked together for the U.S. government's Equal Employment Opportunity Commission (EEOC). In her testimony, Hill claimed that Thomas had repeatedly asked her for dates and spoke to her about pornography and his own sexual prowess. Thomas denied these charges and was eventually confirmed to the Supreme Court. The hearings, televised nationally, generated many television, newspaper, and magazine stories that debated the extent and seriousness of sexual harassment in the United States.

Many experts believe that the media attention devoted to the Hill/Thomas hearings was an appropriate response to an issue that has been long neglected. As *Newsweek* writer Barbara Kantrowitz states, "The publicity surrounding Anita Hill's allegations has brought the issue into the open. . . . It shows that charges of sexual harassment can be taken seriously." The seriousness of sexual harassment is evident, many Americans contend, in the results of a 1991 *New York Times*/CBS News poll that showed that 40 percent of the nation's 55 million working women have experienced some form of sexual harassment. Sexual harassment is not only a serious matter for individual women but also for society as a whole: absenteeism, job turnover, and lost productivity due to sexual harassment cost the U.S. government at least $189 million annually, according to the United States Merit Systems Protection Board.

Lynn Hecht Schafran, an attorney for the National Organization for Women (NOW) Legal Defense and Education Fund, is just one woman who believes the increased media attention led to a much needed increase in awareness of the problem and may spur employers to take action. Schafran states, "The national debate sparked by Professor Hill's allegations has infused women with a new determination to have this issue taken seriously. . . . This national focus on sexual harassment provides an unparalleled opportunity for companies to educate employees on this issue."

Others disagree that the publicity surrounding the Thomas/Hill hearings had such benefits. Some experts believe the media attention obscured and overdramatized the extent of sexual harassment. Confused about what sexual harassment is, workers are distancing themselves from one another, afraid of doing anything that might be misconstrued as sexual harassment. Some employers have become so sensitive to possible sexual harassment lawsuits that they are tense and uncommunicative. *Time* magazine associate editor Nancy Gibbs characterized the suspicious mood following the hearings, stating, "In America's workplaces, men and women reintroduced themselves with a suspicion that their relationships had changed forever. Men who have worked closely with women for years asked them flat out, 'Have you ever felt threatened or insulted or offended by anything I've said or done?'"

This increased tension, some believe, actually threatens equality in the workplace by increasing suspicion and distrust between men and women. In addition, some believe the media blitz surrounding Hill's accusations has frightened many good people from public office. As columnist Joseph Perkins states, "Charges of sexual harassment have become a virtual political death sentence. Are we a better nation for this? . . . Hardly. If anything, honorable people—like Justice Thomas—will be dissuaded in the future from entering public life."

Whether it was unjustified sensationalism or serious journalism, the Hill/Thomas hearings brought the issue of sexual harassment to the forefront of public debate. The long-term effects are still being sorted out a year later. Men and women, employers and employees have begun to address sexual harassment, bringing change—whether positive or negative—to the nation. As *Time* magazine stated, "Too many conversations occurred, too many stories were told, for men and women to return comfortably to old patterns of behavior." Without question, more people are aware of the issue than ever before. The viewpoints in *Sexual Harassment: Current Controversies* reflect this awareness and examine the concern and ambivalence felt by both men and women toward sexual harassment.

Chapter 1

Is Sexual Harassment
a Serious Problem?

CURRENT CONTROVERSIES

Sexual Harassment in America: An Overview

by Barbara Kantrowitz

About the author: *Barbara Kantrowitz is a senior writer for* Newsweek, *a weekly newsmagazine.*

They may be neurosurgeons or typists, police officers or telephone operators, construction workers or even members of Congress. In October 1991 women around the country who disagree on a hundred other issues listened to Anita Hill's allegations and heard themselves talking. They remembered the boss who threatened them, the co-worker whose lewd remarks echoed for hours. They remembered how angry they felt and how they pushed that anger down deep and how they tried to forget—and how they couldn't forget.

A Fact of Life

Sexual harassment is a fact of life in the American workplace; 21 percent of women polled by *Newsweek* said they had been harassed at work and 42 percent said they knew someone who had been harassed. Other surveys indicate that more than half of working women have faced the problem at some point in their careers. The situation tends to be worst in male-dominated workplaces; in a 1990 Defense Department study, 64 percent of military women said they had endured such abuse. Although the severity may vary—from a pattern of obscene joking to outright assault—the emotional damage is often profound and long-lasting. Men "don't understand that caged feeling," says University of Texas sociologist Susan Marshall. "But women know what sexual harassment is. It's when your neck hairs stand up, when you feel like you're being stalked."

Defining sexual harassment is one of the law's newest frontiers. While some of the boundaries have been set by recent decisions, there is still considerable debate over just what constitutes actionable behavior. Most people understand that when a supervisor demands that a woman sleep with him in order to keep her job, he's stepped over the legal line. But what about aggressive flirting? Or off-color conversation? Often, it's a matter of perception. Some women may find such activities offensive; others may just shrug. And men and women may see things very differently. University of Arizona professor Barbara Gutek surveyed 1,200 men and women for a study on harassment. She asked her subjects whether they considered a sexual proposition flattering. About 67 percent of the men said they would, while only 17 percent of the women agreed. In contrast, 63 percent of women would be insulted by a proposition, compared with 15 percent of men.

> *"Until just a few years ago, women had no recourse when confronted with unwanted advances or offensive comments by a boss or co-worker."*

Even when their cases seem clear-cut, women say they feel ashamed—as though they were to blame for what happened to them. "Do we have to talk about the sex?" asks Mitzie Buckelew, as her eyes redden and tears begin to fall. She would like to forget that night with her boss in a suburban Atlanta hotel five years ago. Buckelew has claimed in state and federal lawsuits that Donald Farrar, the DeKalb County assistant police chief, threatened to fire her from her secretarial job if she did not have sex with him. He calls her charges "ludicrous." Buckelew claims that even after she gave in, hoping that would end the abuse, he persisted. "He would sneak up behind me and grab my breasts and my rear end right in the office," she says. "He would feel up and down my legs." Buckelew also claims Farrar gave her herpes; he has refused to give her lawyers his medical records.

Since Buckelew filed a harassment complaint in 1989, her car has been vandalized. Obscene phone calls wake her up in the middle of the night. She's still waiting for a resolution of the state and federal suits she has filed. In the meantime, she's been reassigned: to the county dog pound. Shortly after Buckelew sued, Farrar resigned with a full pension. "You start questioning yourself," Buckelew says. "Maybe I did ask for it. I know I didn't use good judgment . . . I just didn't know what to do."

No Objections

Until just a few years ago, women had no recourse when confronted with unwanted advances or offensive comments by a boss or co-worker. In offices where they were the minority, women thought they had to go along to get along. Palma Formica, a family practitioner in New Jersey, recalls that when she was a medical student more than 30 years ago, it was "standard procedure" for professors to make "male-female jokes, usually genital oriented, with the woman bearing the brunt." Women never objected. "What are you going to do, get up and walk out of class? You want to be a doctor? You want to be in a man's field? Then you swallow hard and pretend you don't hear."

But in the past decade, as women have grown to represent nearly half the work force, the courts have begun to strike down what was once "standard procedure." In 1980, the Equal Employment Opportunity Commission (the federal agency that investigates bias in the workplace) said that making sexual activity a condition of employment or promotion was a violation of the 1964 Civil Rights Act. Also forbidden: the creation of "an intimidating, hostile or offensive working environment."

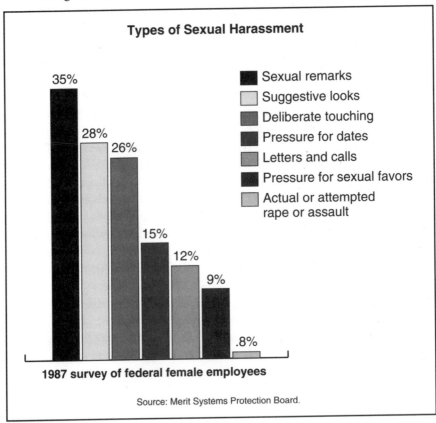

The EEOC rules had little effect on most women's lives until 1986, when the Supreme Court agreed that sexual harassment did indeed violate civil rights. In the landmark case of *Meritor Savings Bank v. Vinson*, Washington, D.C., bank employee Mechelle Vinson claimed that her supervisor fondled her in front of other employees, followed her into the ladies' room, exposed himself and, on several occasions, raped her. The supervisor and the bank denied her claims, but the court sided with Vinson.

Two other major federal court decisions refined the legal definition. In a Florida case involving a female shipyard worker, the court ruled that nude pinups in the workplace constitute illegal harassment. A week later a three-judge panel in San Francisco stated that in cases where men and women might see a pattern of behavior differently, the deciding factor should be whether a "reasonable woman" might feel threatened. In that case, a female IRS worker turned down a request for a date by a co-worker. He responded by writing unwelcome love letters to her. "Men, who are rarely victims of sexual assault, may view sexual conduct in a vacuum without a full appreciation of the underlying threat of violence that a woman may perceive," wrote Judge Robert R. Beezer.

State Standards

States have also been trying to set their own standards. Kent Sezer, general counsel for the Illinois Human Rights Commission, describes one case in that state in which a judge developed what Sezer calls the "stub-your-toe test." An employer had been using profane language; a female employee claimed he had created a hostile environment. The employer said the words were simply expletives and protected as free speech. The judge disagreed. He said that the expletives should be put to a simple test. If the employer had awakened at night and, as he got out of bed, stubbed his toe, would he have shouted, "Oh, cunt!"? The judge didn't think so, and ruled against the employer.

> *"Only about 6 percent of victims file formal complaints."*

These decisions and others have spurred hundreds of public and private employers to write sexual-harassment policies telling workers exactly how to behave. "Nowadays, it's basically a legal requirement that you have an anti-harassment policy," says Joan Engstrom, equal-employment-opportunity director for General Mills (109,000 employees), based in Minneapolis. Courts may hold employers liable for maintaining a harassment-free environment; the bill for failure can be steep. Although many cases are settled out of court and then sealed, there have been several multimillion-dollar awards in recent years. Avoiding huge payments isn't the only incentive for companies (many awards are, in fact, under $10,000). The publicity surrounding a harassment charge can damage a company's standing with the public.

But corporate policies are only as good as the supervisors who enforce them. Freada Klein, who heads a Cambridge, Mass., consulting firm that advises companies on harassment, says that one third of harassers are the victims' immediate supervisors. Another third, she says, are even higher up on the corporate ladder but do not directly supervise their victims. The rest are the victims' peers. Like many companies with well-respected records in this area, General Mills runs regular training sessions for employees, with videos explaining sexual harassment. Engstrom says General Mills tries to give its employees a simple explanation of its policy: "Employees are to be treated with dignity and respect. Unbusinesslike conduct that could be considered offensive or intimidating will not be tolerated."

Other companies have more bureaucratic systems in place. At AT&T, whose national work force is 47 percent female, managers must attend an annual training session that includes a discussion of sexual harassment. Nonmanagers learn about the company policy through a book that explains the company's investigation process. Employees also get a copy of the company's code of conduct and many see training tapes on sexual harassment. Company spokesman Burke Stinson says 95 percent of complaints filed with AT&T's personnel office "turn out to be founded." AT&T officials won't give out exact figures, but they say that some employees have been fired and others transferred or sent to counseling.

> *"Most judges perceive themselves as identifying with the man no matter how horrible he is."*

Even if they work for a company with a well-established harassment policy, many women still keep their mouths shut. They don't want to be seen as troublemakers—and they worry about the long-term consequences of complaining. "The individual who makes the complaint is immediately subjected to scrutiny, criticism and blame," says Carolyn Chalmers, a Minneapolis lawyer who handles harassment cases. "You're immediately put on the defensive to justify your existence and your credibility." It's a rather simple risk-and-reward equation that for many women adds up to one big zero. The number of cases of sexual harassment reported to the EEOC and local bias agencies has increased somewhat in the past few years, from 4,380 in 1984 to 5,694 in 1991. Yet those numbers represent just a tiny fraction of actual incidents, lawyers say. According to Joan Huwiler of the NOW Legal Defense Fund, only about 6 percent of victims file formal complaints to the EEOC, other anti-bias agencies or their employers.

Frances Conley, a neurosurgeon at Stanford Medical School, endured nearly 25 years of insults before she finally quit her job. Her charges of harassment drew national headlines and letters of support from around the country. The university responded by setting up a committee to investigate the charges. Now Conley's back at her job, hoping that things will get better. But the four months since her resignation "have been the worst four months in my life," Conley says. "I hate conflict. I hate people disapproving of me. It's very difficult to go around with people not liking you."

Formidable Obstacles

Women who take their accusations to court face even more formidable obstacles than public disapproval. The legal process is long and cumbersome—it can be years from first complaint to final verdict—and in the interim, the woman is in a legal, professional and often financial limbo. "A woman will complain and then becomes a pariah," says Judith Vladeck, a New York lawyer who has argued anti-bias cases for 20 years. "If the male is in any way sanctioned, his male cohorts come to his defense, and the woman becomes the wrongdoer, and she's frozen out."

Lawyers, too, say the cases are draining. Women are not entitled to collect damages under the Civil Rights Act—just back pay. Often, that's not enough for a lawyer to spend years in litigation. There are larger judgments in civil suits, but the legal proceedings can be time-consuming. Patricia J. Barry, the Los Angeles lawyer who argued the precedent-setting Vinson case before the Supreme Court in 1986, filed for bankruptcy in 1988 and announced she was giving up civil-rights work. Now she's arguing divorce and child-custody cases. "Most judges perceive themselves as identifying with the man no matter how horrible he is," Barry says. "It becomes the woman versus the man."

Dark Victory

Even some of those who win harassment cases say they feel they lost. As a public-information officer for the Illinois Department of Corrections, Lynda Savage earned glowing evaluations and two salary increases in the early 1980s. But, according to court records, her supervisor, Nicholas Howell, commonly used obscenities when referring to women, brought in suggestive lingerie catalogs and asked Savage to pick out something for his wife and even told her she should buy a vibrator for her 1-year-old daughter. Howell denies directing obscene comments to Savage. She complained to three different administrators, but nothing happened. For months, she says, Howell's behavior got worse. She was fired just before her second child was born.

> *"It should be considered illegal harassment when a man makes an obscene comment to a woman in the street."*

Nearly five years later, a state court ruled in her favor and awarded her $137,000, along with an offer of reinstatement to her job. Savage did go back, but says her co-workers shunned her so she quit. She has not received another job offer. "In a lot of ways, I have tested my limits so I know where I'm strong and where I'm not," she says. "Some good has come out of it. But was it worth it?" She thinks about the years of strain on her children and her husband, the lost work opportunities. And she concludes: "No."

Sexual-harassment cases have been particularly controversial on college campuses. A 1986 survey by the Association of American Colleges reported that 32 percent of tenured faculty women at Harvard and 49 percent of untenured women had reported some form of sexual harassment. Consultant Freada Klein says that 40 percent of undergraduate women and 28 percent of female graduate students say they've been harassed. In 1989, the Minnesota Legislature

21

passed a law requiring all educational institutions in the state to develop sexual-harassment policies. "Some universities have gone so far as to indicate that for a faculty member to date a student is a prima facie case of sexual harassment," says Margaret Neale, a professor at Northwestern's Kellogg Graduate School of Management. "There is no way to separate the power of the faculty member from the rank of the student."

Male-dominated campuses, like male-dominated professions, have the most entrenched problems. In early September 1991 a sophomore at Texas A&M University was attacked by three male cadets when she decided to try out for an elite ceremonial unit within the A&M Corps of Cadets. Only three of the unit's 50 members were female. One of the men held her while two others struck her in the breasts and back. One of the attackers threatened her with a knife, dragging the handle against her flesh and warning that he would use the blade on her if she didn't withdraw her application. The university leveled disciplinary charges against 20 cadets, but officials soon found out this was not an isolated incident.

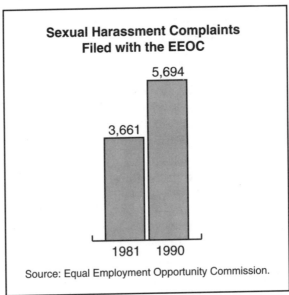

Sexual Harassment Complaints Filed with the EEOC

Source: Equal Employment Opportunity Commission.

Within days A&M president William Mobley met with four women cadets who detailed a pattern of harassment. One woman told Mobley that she had been raped by a senior while his roommate watched. The women got Mobley's attention. He appointed a committee to investigate and named a woman psychologist with no university affiliation to cochair it. "I don't want to destroy the university," says one of the women students who met with Mobley. "But men hide behind the mask of harassment and say it's tradition. That needs to stop."

Some experts believe that "hostile environments" extend far beyond the campus and the workplace. In 1991, 13 female tenants won an $800,000 settlement against their San Francisco landlord who continued to employ an apartment manager even after they repeatedly notified the landlord that the manager was harassing the women. According to court records, the manager touched one woman's vaginal area and grabbed her breast. He told another woman he would evict her if she had an overnight visitor. He told women who were behind on their rent they would have to pay immediately or model lingerie for him. The women, all single mothers, were usually financially or emotionally vulnerable to his manipulations.

While that situation seems extreme, some feminist legal scholars argue that harassment is part of everyday life for most women and should be regulated. Indiana University professor Carol Brooks Gardner, author of a forthcoming book called "Passing By," argues that it should be considered illegal harassment when a man makes an obscene comment to a woman in the street. Of course, not all street comments are threatening. A simple wolf whistle probably wouldn't traumatize most women. "But," says Gardner, "it's not OK for a man to touch me in any way whatsoever or to mutter salacious comments in my ear, or to yell out vulgar verbal evaluations." Any regulations against this type of harassment would be extremely difficult to enforce. For example, who would detain the assailant? Women in such a situation usually just want to get away as quickly as possible.

Honor Roll

Whatever happens on the street or in the courts, the publicity surrounding Anita Hill's allegations brought the issue into the open. "The fact that this claim scuttled the nomination or delayed the nomination helps the cause like nothing else does," says Nancy Gertner, a Boston civil-rights attorney. It shows that charges of sexual harassment can be taken seriously—even in an almost all-male institution like the Senate. In fact, Congress could be the first test of how well the public has been educated by the proceedings. Congressional employees are not covered by the Civil Rights Act, and therefore have no protection against harassment. To correct this oversight, the Women's Political Caucus sent a written policy to all 535 members of Congress. Those who agreed to run harassment-free offices joined the caucus's "Honor Roll.". . . After listening to Anita Hill, a lot of women voters would like to see Congress put its own House—and Senate—in order.

Sexual Harassment Is a Serious Problem

by Anita Hill

About the author: *Anita Hill, a University of Oklahoma law professor, came to the nation's attention in October 1991 when she testified that U.S. Supreme Court nominee Clarence Thomas had sexually harassed her. Hill's testimony sparked a nationwide debate concerning sexual harassment.*

The response to my 1991 Senate Judiciary Committee testimony has been at once heartwarming and heart-wrenching. In learning that I am not alone in experiencing harassment, I am also learning that there are far too many women who have experienced a range of inexcusable and illegal activities—from sexist jokes to sexual assault—on the job.

My reaction has been to try to learn more. As an educator, I always begin to study an issue by examining the scientific data—the articles, the books, the studies. Perhaps the most compelling lesson is in the stories told by the women who have written to me. I have learned much; I am continuing to learn; I have yet ten times as much to explore. I want to share some of this with you.

The Nature of the Beast

Sexual harassment . . . is alive and well. A harmful, dangerous thing that can confront a woman at any time.

What we know about harassment, sizing up the beast:

Sexual harassment is pervasive . . .

1. It occurs today at an alarming rate. Statistics show that anywhere from 42 to 90 percent of women will experience some form of harassment during their employed lives. At least 1 percent experience sexual assault. But the statistics do not fully tell the story of the anguish of women who have been told in various ways on the first day of a job that sexual favors are expected. Or the story of women who were sexually assaulted by men with whom they continued to work.

2. It has been occurring for years. In letters to me, women tell of incidents that occurred 50 years ago when they were first entering the workplace, incidents they have been unable to speak of for that entire period.

3. Harassment crosses lines of race and class. In some ways, it is a creature that practices "equal opportunity" where women are concerned. In other ways it exhibits predictable prejudices and reflects stereotypical myths held by our society.

We know that harassment all too often goes unreported for a variety of reasons . . .

1. Unwillingness (for good reason) to deal with the expected consequences;
2. Self-blame;
3. Threats or blackmail by coworkers or employers;
4. What it boils down to in many cases is a sense of powerlessness that we experience in the workplace, and our acceptance of a certain level of inability to control our careers and professional destinies. This sense of powerlessness is particularly troubling when one observes the research that says individuals with graduate education experience more harassment than do persons with less than a high school diploma. The message: when you try to obtain power through education, the beast harassment responds by striking more often and more vehemently.

A Dirty Secret

That harassment is treated like a woman's "dirty secret" is well known. We also know what happens when we "tell." We know that when harassment is reported the common reaction is disbelief or worse . . .

1. Women who "tell" lose their jobs. A typical response told of in the letters to me was: I not only lost my job for reporting harassment, but I was accused of stealing and charges were brought against me.

2. Women who "tell" become emotionally wasted. One writer noted that "it was fully eight months after the suit was conducted that I began to see myself as alive again."

3. Women who "tell" are not always supported by other women. Perhaps the most disheartening stories I have received are of mothers not believing daughters. In my kindest moments I believe that this reaction only represents attempts to distance ourselves from the pain of the harassment experience. The internal response is: "It didn't happen to me. This couldn't happen to me. In order to believe that I am protected, I must believe that it didn't

> *"Anywhere from 42 to 90 percent of women will experience some form of harassment during their employed lives."*

happen to her." The external response is: "What did you do to provoke that kind of behavior?" Yet at the same time that I have been advised of hurtful and unproductive reactions, I have also heard stories of mothers and daughters sharing their experiences. In some cases the sharing allows for a closer bonding. In others a slight but cognizable mending of a previously damaged relationship occurs.

What we are learning about harassment requires recognizing this beast when we encounter it, and more. It requires looking the beast in the eye.

We are learning painfully that simply having laws against harassment on the books is not enough. The law, as it was conceived, was to provide a shield of protection for us. Yet that shield is failing us: many fear reporting, others feel it would do no good.

> *"Women who 'tell' are not always supported by other women."*

The result is that less than 5 percent of women victims file claims of harassment. Moreover, the law focuses on quid pro quo, but a recent *New York Times* article quoting psychologist Dr. Louise Fitzgerald says that this makes up considerably less than 5 percent of the cases. The law needs to be more responsive to the reality of our experiences.

As we are learning, enforcing the law alone won't terminate the problem. What we are seeking is equality of treatment in the workplace. Equality requires an expansion of our attitudes toward workers. Sexual harassment denies our treatment as equals and replaces it with treatment of women as objects of ego or power gratification. Dr. John Gottman, a psychologist at the University of Washington, notes that sexual harassment is more about fear than about sex.

Yet research suggests two troublesome responses exhibited by workers and by courts. Both respond by . . .

1. Downplaying the seriousness of the behavior (seeing it as normal sexual attraction between people) or commenting on the sensitivity of the victim.

2. Exaggerating the ease with which victims are expected to handle the behavior. But my letters tell me that unwanted advances do not cease—and that the message was power, not genuine interest.

Women Are Angry

We are learning that many women are angry. The reasons for the anger are various and perhaps all too obvious . . .

1. We are angry because this awful thing called harassment exists in terribly harsh, ugly, demeaning, and even debilitating ways. Many believe it is criminal and should be punished as such. It is a form of violence against women as well as a form of economic coercion, and our experiences suggest that it won't just go away.

2. We are angry because for a brief moment we believed that if the law allowed for women to be hired in the workplace, and if we worked hard for our educations and on the job, equality would be achieved. We believed we would be respected as equals. Now we are realizing this is not true. We have been betrayed. The reality is that this powerful beast is used to perpetuate a sense of in-

equality, to keep women in their place notwithstanding our increasing presence in the workplace.

What we have yet to explore about harassment is vast. It is what will enable us to slay the beast.

Research is helpful, appreciated, and I hope will be required reading for all legislators. Yet research has what I see as one shortcoming: it focuses on our re-action to harassment, not on the harasser. How we enlighten men who are currently in the workplace about behavior that is beneath our (and their) dignity is the challenge of the future. Research shows that men tend to have a narrower definition of what constitutes harassment than do women. How do we expand their body of knowledge? How do we raise a generation of men who won't need to be reeducated as adults? We must explore these issues, and research efforts can assist us.

What are the broader effects of harassment on women and the world? Has sexual harassment left us unempowered? Has our potential in the workplace been greatly damaged by this beast? Has this form of economic coercion worked? If so, how do we begin to reverse its effects? We must begin to use what we know to move to the next step: what we will do about it.

How do we capture our rage and turn it into positive energy? Through the power of women working together, whether it be in the political arena, or in the context of a lawsuit, or in community service. This issue goes well beyond partisan politics. Making the workplace a safer, more productive place for ourselves and our daughters should be on the agenda for each of us. It is something we can do for ourselves. It is a tribute, as well, to our mothers—and indeed a contribution we can make to the entire population.

> *"Making the workplace a safer, more productive place for ourselves and our daughters should be on the agenda for each of us."*

I wish that I could take each of you on the journey that I've been on since the hearing. I wish that every one of you could experience the heartache and the triumphs of each of those who have shared with me their experiences. I leave you with but a brief glimpse of what I've seen. I hope it is enough to encourage you to begin—or continue and persist with—your own exploration.

Sexual Harassment Is a Serious Problem at Universities

by Marilyn Gaye Piety

About the author: *Marilyn Gaye Piety, a Fulbright scholar, is a doctoral student in philosophy at a university in Denmark.*

Shortly after I arrived at a prestigious eastern university to complete the work for my Ph.D., one of the professors in the department began to harass me. This harassment consisted of repeated requests for dates as well as sexually suggestive remarks made to me both in private and in front of other professors in the department. This went on for several weeks.

I made a point of procuring a copy of the university regulations concerning sexual harassment, but I was surprised to discover that there was no university prohibition on sexual relations between professors and students. Students were considered "adults" by the university and, therefore, capable of informed "consent" to such relationships. As long as this professor's repeated requests for dates were phrased politely and involved no overt threat to my situation as a student in the department, they did not fall under the heading of behavior that was prohibited.

Formal Complaint Discouraged

After several weeks of fending off the advances of this professor (whom I shall refer to as Bill), I turned to the chairman of the department for help. When I explained my situation to him, he seemed sympathetic. But, despite the fact that he admitted I was not the first student Bill had treated this way, he discouraged me from making a *formal* complaint. While he assured me that Bill's behavior was unacceptable, he was certain that it was not maliciously motivated. I would not want, he said, to risk the possibility of doing him any professional

Marilyn Gaye Piety, "Sexual Harassment on Campus," *Christian Social Action*, July/August 1991.
Reprinted with permission.

injury by making a *formal* complaint against him. He suggested that perhaps the best thing to do would be for him to have a "talk" with Bill.

I was anxious to resolve the problem without harming this person whose actions, for all their damaging nature, may not have been malicious. I did not consider that the chairman must have talked with Bill before, that the talk had clearly been ineffectual, and that there was no reason to believe it would work this time.

After I spoke to the chairman, Bill stopped asking me for dates, so I assumed that my problem had been solved. I was informed, however, by another professor (who could have gotten in considerable trouble with the university for revealing this information to me) that Bill repeatedly made disparaging remarks about my work and intelligence in closed faculty meetings. As a result the faculty was becoming so prejudiced against me that there was a very real chance I would not receive any financial support for the coming academic year, she indicated.

Counselors with No Real Authority

This university, like many, has counselors specifically appointed to handle complaints of sexual harassment. In desperation, I went to one of these counselors and explained my situation. She was distressed by my story, but I was shocked to discover that she had no real authority to do anything about it. The most she could do was suggest to the department, or to the university, that something should be done, but ultimately either of these authorities had to decide whether and how to act on her suggestion. They never did.

Students who become the objects of romantic attentions of a professor are often caught in a see-saw of emotions. They are sometimes unsure whether their situation would actually be considered "harassment," but they almost always feel exceptionally vulnerable and experience a desire to strike out at the source. . . .

It is very difficult to get statistics on the proportion of students harassed by professors because, as one sexual harassment counselor explained, "[m]ost of the cases are handled informally without going to court or to a public forum." Thus, no records of these cases are kept. It is not even possible to get a picture of the average case of harassment because complaints of harassment are usually confidential. This confidentiality is often interpreted by the counselor as meaning that no details concerning these cases may be revealed.

One might legitimately wonder why all the secrecy? Surely a counselor could release general information concerning the form most sexual harassment takes without violating the confidentiality of particular cases. The answer behind the secrecy is that many universities simply do not want the pervasiveness of sexual harassment on their

> *"Students who become the objects of romantic attentions of a professor are often caught in a see-saw of emotions."*

campuses to be exposed.

Harassment very seldom comes in the form of overt threats or promises and yet that is how it is often defined in university policies. The kind of harassment, most commonly based on my research and interviews with both graduate and undergraduate students, as well as established scholars, seldom involves such overt threats. The absence of threats, however, only makes this harassment more, not less, dangerous and destructive. That is, it leaves the student in a vulnerable position, afraid to confide his or her problem for fear of being labeled "paranoid."

Often, an investigation of any alleged harassment can only be undertaken "if the complainant agrees to be identified." But imagine an insecure college freshman agreeing to be identified as bringing a complaint of harassment against a professor who has not even overtly threatened him or her! It almost never happens, and universities hope that the absence of such formal complaints will be interpreted by the public as reflecting an absence of harassment.

Policies Protect Universities and Employees

Sexual harassment policies are, more often than not, set up to protect universities and their employees—that is, the *harassers* rather than the *harassees*. This has been allowed to happen because good people have consistently sent the message to universities that they do not care to know what goes on within their walls. The only time most people ever really come to appreciate the inadequacy of more university policies on sexual harassment is when they, or someone they know,

"Many universities simply do not want the pervasiveness of sexual harassment on their campuses to be exposed."

have become victims of it, and then it is too late. One professor I spoke to, who was also the chairman of his department, explained that few professors in his department were completely free of the stain of such harassment. Thus, when a particularly bad case arose, he was unable to get any of the other professors to support the victim because they were so afraid that the accused would turn around and point the finger at them.

There is no formal record anywhere that Bill has ever sexually harassed a student, let alone that he is a chronic harasser. He has now taken a job at another university, but his behavior has not changed. Several months ago I received a letter from the sexual harassment counselor with whom I had spoken at Bill's former university asking if I would be willing to support a woman whom Bill was harassing at this new university. It seemed this woman was considering making a formal complaint against Bill. However, to make a strong case, she needed the testimony of other women he had harassed.

Unfortunately, this woman eventually decided *not* to make a formal complaint. She explained that she was afraid of stirring up trouble and possibly prejudicing the rest of the faculty against her by taking such an action. The difficulty is that her fears were well-founded. Faculties do not like students who make trouble. Even if her complaint was ultimately successful—i.e., even if it eventuated in some censure of Bill—she might never again receive any professional support from anyone on the faculty of her department.

> *"Many schools still do not have a formal policy prohibiting the sexual harassment of students."*

It would appear that the concern of the university is not with the emotional or even professional well-being of its students and graduate students. It is a disappointing thing to realize, but it should not be any great surprise. . . .

Many schools still do not have a formal policy prohibiting the sexual harassment of students. Furthermore, many existing policies are inadequate; therefore, it is important to read any information from the schools quite carefully. If the policy in question indicates that harassment must involve *overt* threats or promises of reward, it is inadequate. If it only allows an investigation into reported cases of harassment when the victim agrees to be identified, it is inadequate.

Professors' Rights Are Primary

No one wants academe to be given over to witch hunts where any anonymous allegation of impropriety can ruin a career. The fact is, however, that under many existing sexual harassment policies, the professors' rights are far more well protected than the students. One formal complaint of impropriety is far from enough to get a tenured professor dismissed.

However, one instance of such "impropriety" can be enough to injure a student *substantially*. It can cause a considerable degree of emotional distress and can demoralize the student to the extent that his or her grades will suffer. Perhaps more importantly, it can create a fear and suspicion of authority that may stay with the student for the rest of his or her life.

If the school from which parents have requested information (and they may request this information in person as well as in writing) either does not have a policy concerning sexual harassment or has an inadequate policy, anyone can exert pressure on the school to draft such a policy or to revise existing policy. A person can do this by expressing concern to both the dean of the college or university in question and to local newspapers.

Persons who attended a college or university may exert considerable pressure upon the institution by suggesting that they will discontinue support if the school does not adopt a responsible sexual harassment policy and by informing the school that they will encourage other alumni to do the same. Church persons can put similar pressure on church-related colleges and universities. Most colleges and universities are responsive to public concerns—if those concerns are made apparent to them—because so much of their funding comes from the public. So few people, however, really *know* what goes on in most colleges and universities. That is why sexual harassment on college and university campuses is so pervasive.

The best thing for students to do if they find, or even suspect, that they are the object of such harassment (and this is advice every church ought to provide for its young members as well as other individuals in the community) is to make some record of the relevant event or events. This record does not have to be elaborate; a note or two jotted down in a calendar on the date of the event is enough. Such a record will help to lessen the anxiety that the event may have caused. If the student is lucky, there will be no more events to record and the note will simply be forgotten. However, if there is another event, even something as apparently innocent as a professor standing uncomfortably close to the student in a line or in the hall, it should be recorded. In this way it becomes possible to establish whether a pattern is emerging.

If such a pattern becomes evident, the student should go to see a university counselor. Again, many universities have counselors who are appointed specifically to talk to students who have complaints about sexual harassment. If a particular university does not have such counselors, it will have counselors appointed to deal with other student problems such as depression and test-anxiety, and the student may speak to one of them.

There is no risk involved in seeing a counselor. The counselor will simply listen to the student's story and give advice on how to pursue the matter. It is important to remember, however, that these counselors are often under pressure from their college or university to seek an *informal* solution to the problem and that such informal solutions are often unsatisfactory.

Students Need Support

Apart from exerting pressure upon various colleges and universities to adopt responsible sexual harassment policies, one of the most important things we can do is to encourage young people to be open about such experiences and to support them when they do confide in us. Students need our support because the subtlety of most harassment often leaves them feeling confused, vulnerable, and even guilty.

> *"The subtlety of most harassment often leaves [students] feeling confused, vulnerable, and even guilty."*

Several students to whom I spoke actually confided to their parents or to other adults that they were being made "uncomfortable" by the behavior of one of their professors. They found, however, that they received little support. Unfortunately, we are sometimes inclined to characterize the vague feelings often expressed by victims of harassment as expressions of paranoia and thus ultimately the problem of the student rather than of the professor or the college or university. We need to assure students that it may not be their fault if they feel "uncomfortable" around a particular professor and that we will support them if they decide to make a formal complaint. . . .

It is time we accepted the responsibility for reacting to this pervasive injustice. Although more subtle than other injustices, it is not less devastating to its victims.

Sexual Harassment Is a Serious Problem in the Financial Industry

by Laurie P. Cohen, William Power, and Michael Siconolfi

About the authors: *Laurie P. Cohen, William Power, and Michael Siconolfi are staff reporters for the* Wall Street Journal.

It's official: Wall Street is declaring war on sexism.

Several of the country's most august financial institutions, jolted by the furor surrounding the confirmation of Associate Supreme Court Justice Clarence Thomas, have issued unusual gender-sensitive decrees.

In a firm-wide letter, the chairman of Merrill Lynch & Co. warned that the nation's biggest brokerage firm would "not tolerate any form of sexual harassment." Morgan Stanley Group Inc., Bear Stearns Cos., Prudential Securities Inc., Salomon Brothers Inc. and First Boston Corp. have all issued similar warnings. Even the little Coffee, Sugar & Cocoa Exchange is reviewing its policies.

Old-Boy Customs

But there is both good news and bad news behind such well-intentioned pronouncements: Wall Street offers women some of the best opportunities in America for reaping huge financial rewards, power and prominence, and pays lip-service to an ethic of equal opportunity. But at the same time, as the new warnings from management suggest, the industry remains subject to old-boy customs that many women see as a hindrance, from their first raunchy hazing until their final bump against the still-fixed glass ceiling.

The coffee exchange's campaign against sexism illustrates the persistence of the problem. Although the exchange decreed that "all inappropriate pictures, pinups and postcards" featuring nude women were to be removed from the trading floor, yesterday pinups of bare breasts were still stapled to the walls of some traders' booths, in full view of the men and women who dart about the exchange floor. Asked about this, an exchange senior vice president, James Bowe, artfully notes that in the three-quarters of the trading booths he checked at least, there was only "one postcard with girls in bikinis on it." Ludicrous though such prudish policing may seem, the point, say many who work there, is that despite the most high-minded pronouncements, the gap between policy and practice remains wide on Wall Street.

To be sure, Wall Street's record may be no worse than that of corporate America as a whole, and in fact, the Street is one of the few arenas in which a woman with enough drive and skill can break into the seven-figure income bracket.

Slow Climb Up Ladder

But while women have indisputably made gains in the financial world over the past 20 years, statistics suggest that their climb to the top has been slow. Women hold 40% of the jobs at Wall Street's 10 largest securities firms, but they make up just 4% of all partners and managing directors—these firms' most coveted and highly paid positions, according to a *Wall Street Journal* survey. At

"The gap between policy and practice remains wide on Wall Street."

Goldman, Sachs & Co., Wall Street's most successful investment bank, just four of the 146 partners are women. At the New York Stock Exchange, only two of the 26 directors are women.

And such numbers only hint at the kinds of subtle discrimination many women say they still face, from the first day of job interviews to the assignments they get—often in less glamorous areas such as securities and economic research and municipal finance—to the salaries they take home. More than many industries, the brokerage business is based on personal relationships, steeped in prankish humor, and reliant on clannish favor-swapping. Whether deals are clinched on the golf course or in the deep leather chairs of New York's hoary and, until recently, all-male clubs, the Old Boys, say many women, still hold the advantage.

Not all women agree, and in fact, some say their experience has been quite the opposite. Elaine Garzarelli, Shearson Lehman Brothers Inc.'s top-rated stock-market strategist and one of Wall Street's best-known women, says she hasn't had any discrimination problems.

The Benefits

"I think it's helped me being a woman, actually, on Wall Street," Ms. Garzarelli says. While women may have problems on trading desks, she says, in the research departments "the men seem to respect us as doing a very tedious job and really looking at the details. Women tend to do that. . . . Women are very service-oriented."

Ms. Garzarelli also suggests that women present fewer ego problems for their bosses. She says women "get a bonus and say 'Thank you,' and men say 'Whadaya mean? I deserve more.'" For women on Wall Street, "If you're good and you're smart, you get respect."

But others suggest that in less beneficial ways, from the start, many female job applicants are subjected to different questions than their male counterparts, often reflecting employers' concerns that they might eventually favor families over their firms. In one particularly egregious case a few years ago, a Stanford University student said that a Goldman Sachs recruiter, Michael Werner, asked if she would "have an abortion to save [her] job." Mr. Werner, who is no longer at Goldman, says he merely asked students whether they would advise a friend to have an abortion, to see whether they would "go to the end of the world to be a professional." Goldman says the question was "appalling" and it disciplined Mr. Werner at the time.

Usually, however, Wall Street recruiters are a bit more subtle. "Companies want to know why a woman isn't married, or if she is, why she'd want to spend so much time traveling," says Gary Goldstein, president of Whitney Group, an executive search firm specializing in the financial-services industry.

Once on the job, Wall Street women report an amazing range of offensive and even discriminatory practices, ranging from the mundane to the bizarre. One Wall Street investment banker, for instance, says she discovered she had been promised romantically to the principal in a deal her boss was hoping to snag. The woman, like nearly every woman interviewed with such grievances, asks not to be identified.

Intentional Offenses

Sometimes, the offensive behavior seems almost designed to make a female employee uncomfortable. One woman lawyer tells of a meeting with a senior executive of Oppenheimer in the mid-1980s. After 45 minutes, and in the presence of others, the executive said, "You should have told me to turn down the air conditioning. Your nipples are sticking out." The lawyer says she was both embarrassed and angry, but didn't respond. Another woman at the firm who was present confirms the incident.

> *"Many female job applicants are subjected to different questions than their male counterparts."*

Frequently, female employees feel it too risky to their careers to complain, let alone press charges. Lawyers who represent Wall Street women in sex discrimination cases say that it is a rare woman who will stand up and publicly charge she has been harassed. "You really do get blackballed in the securities industry," says Boston lawyer Beville May. "It's such an old-boys' network."

But when one former Merrill Lynch broker in Boston, Teresa Contardo, took her case to court, she won a landmark victory, remarkable in its description of the kinds of pervasive but subtle discrimination she had faced. After ordering Merrill to pay $250,000 in punitive damages for habitually discriminating against Mrs. Contardo, U.S. District Judge Walter Skinner said in a blistering opinion: "There existed in the office a male 'locker room' atmosphere in which the male brokers engaged in

> *"Frequently, female employees feel it too risky to their careers to complain, let alone press charges."*

lewd remarks and male birthdays were celebrated in the office, in the presence of customers, with . . . a birthday cake in the shape of a phallus." Merrill says it was "disappointed" with the decision, but didn't appeal it.

While subtle put-downs seem commonplace, some women complain that crude sexual harassment still thrives, despite recent efforts by Wall Street firms to stamp it out. As of October 1991, according to the Equal Employment Opportunity Commission, a record 153 cases alleging sexual harassment had been filed against financial institutions, including securities firms, up 50% from the 102 in 1990—an increase that could simply reflect greater awareness of the possibility of legal remedies. Many more cases are settled through arbitration or quietly settled by brokerage firms' lawyers.

Lynn Jennings, a former administrative manager in Atlanta at J.C. Bradford & Co., says she was fired after a series of incidents involving a broker in her office, beginning when the broker grabbed her head "and pulled it toward his crotch." Ms. Jennings, who sued her former employer, says she was subjected to a "virtual campaign of harassment."

For instance, Ms. Jennings said in the suit, filed in Georgia state court, that at a lunch for brokers at the firm's Atlanta office, broker Mark Hill invited her to "get on the table and lie down," allegedly adding, "I bet you'd love that."

A. Lee Parks, Mr. Hill's attorney, denies Ms. Jennings's allegations, and argues that "everyone was laughing about the gigantic bowls of potato salad and cole slaw, which were so big you could roll around in them." The lawyer says that "no one took [Mr. Hill's comments] as sexual harassment."

Wall Street Harassment

Even before the recent pronouncements from the top firms regarding their commitment to fighting sexual harassment, Wall Street has taken some steps in recent years to recruit more women and promote some of them. Yet "Wall Street is a women-unfriendly environment," says Barbara Roberts, a former capital markets executive and director of Dean Witter Reynolds Inc., who left the indusdustry and now heads the Financial Women's Association of New York. "If you're not comfortable with a certain level of lewdness, you shouldn't be there."

But the larger issue, many women on Wall Street say, is that some of the men who run the firms simply don't believe that women belong in high-powered jobs there. In a 1989 article in *M* magazine, James Cayne, Bear Stearns's president, opined that there weren't many women selling stocks and bonds because, faced with rejection, a Wall Street woman would "probably have to go to the ladies' room and dab her eyes." Now, an apologetic Mr. Cayne says Bear Stearns is "100% committed" to equal opportunity for women; like the other firms, Bear Stearns "reiterated" its anti-harassment policies.

Some Wall Street executives claim women are largely to blame for their unequal status. One chief executive says that his firm was losing nearly 50% of the women it hired out of business school and sought to promote, compared with only 4% of the men. He commissioned a study to determine why. The women, he concluded, "made life-style decisions," a euphemism for having children and working fewer hours. "The cost of training someone is high, and you might be more reluctant to invest in a lot of women," he says.

"Are there special considerations for a woman? Of course there are," says John Chalsty, chief executive of Donaldson, Lufkin & Jenrette Inc. "But if a woman is good enough, we're going to live with those. We've had a number of women here who've left for a while, had children and arranged their lives so they can handle dual careers." Mr. Chalsty himself has two daughters who gave up successful Wall Street careers.

Efforts to Promote Women

And of course, there have been breakthroughs in the 24 years since Muriel Siebert forged her way onto the New York Stock Exchange's all-male roster, becoming its first female member.

In 1991's ranking of Wall Street's securities analysts published by *Institutional Investor* magazine, women won 16% of the top spots. Women analysts won 22 of the 51 positions gained by American Express Co.'s Shearson Lehman Brothers unit in the magazine's widely followed ranking. But there are still no women in Shearson's executive management group. (The firm is "now beginning to develop a cadre of [women] who can move up," says personnel director Rusty Myer, Shearson's highest-ranking woman.)

> *"Wall Street is a women-unfriendly environment."*

Success for Wall Street women is becoming "a more normal thing rather than the exception," says Abby Joseph Cohen, a prominent Goldman market strategist who is the firm's most visible woman. As for discrimination, she says, Wall Street is "too competitive a business to allow that kind of stuff to go on."

But Mrs. Cohen says that isn't the way it always was on Wall Street. She recalls an analysts' meeting early in her career at New York's staid University Club, when the doorman let all the men in but stopped her in her tracks. He said women weren't allowed. Mrs. Cohen told the doorman she was going inside anyway. "If you want to stop me, go ahead," she told him.

Mrs. Cohen was the only female analyst to attend the meeting that day.

Other women analysts say they are offended that analyst meetings continue to be held at the University Club, which allows women now after losing a court fight.

Women Must Be Better

Those who have made it to the top on Wall Street, like Salomon Brothers managing director Jessica Palmer, who heads Salomon's big capital markets group, say that they have faced challenges along the way that their male counterparts didn't. "Does a chief executive want to take advice from a petite woman?" Mrs. Palmer asks, answering her own question. "Not unless she's really good—better than her male colleagues."

Mrs. Siebert, whose firm employs 50 people and is the largest women-owned brokerage house, sums it up this way: "Sure, we've made progress, but we still have a long way to go before Wall Street is a pro-women place."

Robin Spaman, a former Prudential broker, is a case in point. After she opened some 400 new accounts in 1989, she says that male co-workers buzzed that "the reason I opened so many accounts was because I gave free sex with every account." Indignant, Mrs. Spaman notes, "I'm a grandmother!" and then adds, "and frankly, I never did that."

Sexual Harassment Is a Serious Problem in the U.S. Navy

by Kay Krohne

About the author: *Kay Krohne, a retired navy commander, is the author of* The Effect of Sexual Harassment on Female Naval Officers: A Phenomenological Study, *from which this viewpoint is excerpted.*

Sexual harassment is a form of sex discrimination that violates Title VII of the Civil Rights Act of 1964. It is generally defined as unwelcome sexual advances, requests for sexual favors, or other sexually oriented verbal or physical conduct which explicitly or implicitly affects an individual's employment; unreasonably interferes with an individual's work performance; or creates an intimidating, hostile, or offensive work environment.

It is a widespread problem in business, government, academia, and the military with serious personal and organizational consequences. As was evidenced by the widely watched October 1991 hearings to confirm Judge Clarence Thomas to the U.S. Supreme Court, the topic of sexual harassment is of great concern to many Americans. It is also a topic of great confusion among many men and women.

Several Levels of Harassment Exist

The definition of sexual harassment has evolved slowly over the past decade and now encompasses much more than a demand for sex as a term or condition of working. Several levels of harassment have been identified, progressing from workplace displays of sexually oriented posters through sexual teasing, jokes, and remarks to physical touching and assault. Although initially recognized as a workplace problem in the late 1970s, sexual harassment was not often litigated due to the problem of proving to the court that a request for sexual favors had

Excerpted from Kay Krohne, "The Effect of Sexual Harassment on Female Naval Officers: A Phenomenological Study," doctoral dissertation, 1991. Reprinted with permission.

been accompanied by threats of reprisal for noncompliance.

In the eyes of the law, compliance with sexual conduct had to be an explicit condition of employment for an employee to successfully take legal action. In June 1986, the Supreme Court made a pivotal ruling in a sexual harassment case by determining that subjection to an intimidating, hostile, or offensive working environment constituted another form of illegal sex discrimination. This finding created a whole new area of liability for employers as the courts aligned themselves with Equal Employment Opportunity Commission'(EEOC) guidelines which had been published 6 years earlier.

These guidelines remain the most widely used direction for employers in policy development. However, it is important to note that both the EEOC guidelines and most court opinions acknowledge the significance of individual interpretations regarding what actually constitutes sexual harassment. It is defined as *unwelcome* sexual behavior; what is unwelcome by one may not be unwelcome by another. Because it can be defined differently by different people, studies such as this take on added importance.

The occurrence of sexual harassment in the workplace has continued to increase for two main reasons: The rise in the number of women in the workforce, and the movement of women into occupations previously dominated by men. In recent years, sexual harassment has been a frequent subject of litigation as well as a popular subject for social science research. This viewpoint specifically addresses the impact of sexual harassment on women officers in the United States Navy. However, it is equally relevant to other military and civilian organizations, particularly those which are male-dominated and employ women in managerial positions.

The Problem

In 1990, the Defense Manpower Data Center completed a survey on the incidence of sexual harassment in the military. According to the results, 64% of the women surveyed had experienced some form of sexual harassment during the previous 12-month period. A variety of behaviors were recounted including relatively mild forms of harassment such as sexually oriented verbal remarks, and more severe forms of harassment such as requests for quid pro quo sexual favors. In the latter circumstance, sexual advances are directly linked to an employee's employment or advancement.

> *"[S]exual harassment . . . is defined as* **unwelcome** *sexual* **behavior; what is unwelcome by one may not be unwelcome by another."**

The survey conducted by the Defense Manpower Data Center took over 2 years to complete and summarized the responses of 20,400 men and women on active duty. Their replies to survey questions made it clear that the military's efforts in eradicating sexual harassment have simply not been effective. The military has instituted numerous recommended, and even mandated, training programs aimed at education and prevention. Despite this, the percentage of women reporting sexual harassment in the active duty military services was one of the highest in the nation, exceeding that recorded for the Federal Government by over 22%.

> *"The military's efforts in eradicating sexual harassment have simply not been effective."*

Department of Defense policy prohibiting sexual harassment statements have been issued since 1980. Each military service has followed suit with a policy statement of its own. Yet, as late as October 1990, the Department of Defense unveiled another new program aimed at eradication of sexual harassment. These fresh efforts are intended to more clearly specify unacceptable behaviors and to improve the education of military members on current policies as well as the consequences of noncompliance. Despite all these official attempts to resolve this issue, sexual harassment, both mild and severe, continues to be an occupational hazard for women in the military.

Difficulties Faced by Military Women

As movingly stated by Dorothy Schneider and Carl J. Schneider in their book *Sound Off! American Military Women Speak Out* (1988):

> Servicemen and servicewomen work together, they socialize together, and sometimes they live in the same barracks or quarters. They have a lot in common and often enjoy each other's company. Not always. For some women the military is a disastrous experience, a place of harassment and unhappiness, which violates their ideals and principles, where they dread going to work, where no one effectively helps or understands. (p. 78)

Whereas men are fulfilling a cultural ideal as they proudly don their uniforms and march off to defend their nation, Schneider and Schneider point out that a woman often

> must waste the energy that men can save for their jobs or for their pleasures in proving herself, in smashing stereotypes and overcoming prejudice, in coping with men's questions and problems about her sexual identity and her gender roles. She must fritter away time and vigor in dealing with the question, spoken, or unspoken: "Why won't you go to bed with me?" (p. 79)

The high level of reported harassment in the uniformed services is one indication that potential contributions of women to the military mission may have been stunted by a predominantly male environment where women are often viewed more as sex objects than as professional military members. Women who feel harassed are sufficient in number to cause a tremendous amount of disruption in the workplace. Poor morale, absenteeism, low productivity, and litigation are all disruptive and costly aspects of sexual harassment. As a result, a substantial number of tax dollars set aside for the nation's defense have instead been spent on the hidden costs of dealing with this issue.

Compared to the other military services, the Navy has been particularly affected by sexual harassment and its aftermath. Over the past several years, numerous media reports of harassment, both at the Naval Academy and at a Naval Training Center in Florida, have severely tarnished the Navy's public image. In calling for a Congressional investigation into the Florida incident, Senator Sam Nunn, D-Ga., was quoted as saying:

> I am very concerned about the persistent problems the Navy appears to have with the treatment of its women sailors. That such behavior is not dealt with more seriously than documented in the Navy Inspector General's report suggests that there may be institutional problems in the Navy in its treatment of women.

The results of a Navy-wide study on the progress of women initially conducted in 1987 and updated in 1990 reported that most women in the naval service had been victims of sexual harassment and nearly all had observed some form of it.

The military services as a whole and the Navy, in specific, have institutionalized nearly every recommendation currently suggested by the literature to prevent sexual harassment without substantially reducing its incidence. The Navy has straightforward policies and required training programs. It has established a grievance procedure which includes a direct hot line to the inspector general as an alternative to reporting the incident through the chain of command. Training on prevention has been mandatory since 1988, but the Navy's mandated training programs have not been able to overcome years of socialization where men are taught to see women as sexual objects and women are taught to be understanding, compassionate, and yielding to the forceful, assertive, dominant male.

"Sexual harassment, both mild and severe, continues to be an occupational hazard for women in the military."

Officers Also Harassed

Although sexual harassment is statistically a much greater problem for enlisted women, female naval officers are not immune from harassment. In a survey conducted by the Navy in 1989, 26% of the 849 female naval officers surveyed reported they had been harassed in the previous one-year period. In a 1988 survey of female naval officers attending a professional seminar in San Diego, 64% (32 of 52) of the respondents had experienced some type of sexual harassment.

As of October 1990, women officers made up 10.8% of the United States Navy officer corps and numbered slightly in excess of 8,000. These officers perform a myriad of duties ranging from the various administrative tasks of a general unrestricted line officer to warfare specialties such as pilot or surface warfare officer (ship driver). Women officers also serve as nurses, attorneys, chaplains, and dentists. They specialize in such fields as aerospace mainte-nance, civil engineering, and intelli-gence. They are in the front lines of every occupation in the Navy except the submarine and special warfare communities or SEALs.

> *"Most women in the naval service had been victims of sexual harassment and nearly all had observed some form of it."*

Upon her commissioning, each woman officer is welcomed to the Navy with a certificate stating that she, like her male counterparts, serves "at the pleasure of the President." This means that she cannot quit her job or go on strike if she is unhappy with the working environment. If she wishes to leave the Navy, she must resign her commission. Although resignation requests are normally honored, they take time and can be rejected.

Working conditions which become intolerable in a service environment must generally be endured or confronted. A female naval officer must learn to deal with a man who believes women do not belong in uniform and who may use sexual intimidation as a weapon to subjugate her. How does a well-educated, highly trained, professional female naval officer handle a superior who forces unwanted sexual attention on her? She cannot quit. The only remaining options are to (a) confront the harasser and hope that reprisals do not result; (b) report the behavior and hope that reprisals do not result; or (c) tolerate the conduct. . . .

Virtue and Honor Still Valued

The Navy has certain expectations of its Commanding Officers, Executive Officers, and others in authority. A call to virtue, honor, patriotism, and subor-dination to superiors in the chain of command has been made by great naval leaders since John Paul Jones. Some may feel that since the Navy has broken with tradition by recruiting women into what was once "this man's Navy," the exhortations of Jones and his successors no longer have meaning. Virtue and honor, however, do not go out of style and patriotism and subordination are necessary in an organization which is expected to defend the nation and its con-stitution.

If those in authority were to "guard against and suppress all dissolute and im-moral practices" as Navy regulations would have them do, there would be no need for a study [on sexual harassment]. Unfortunately, that has not happened. In the words of Admiral Carlisle Trost, former Chief of Naval Operations, in March 1988:

Recent Navy and DoD studies indicate that various forms of sexual harassment (particularly verbal abuse) are far too prevalent. The studies found leadership frequently unaware of the extent of sexual harassment within their commands, training programs ineffective, and procedures for reporting instances of sexual harassment not understood and lacking the confidence of our people.

It is time for a new approach to the issue. Attitudes must change. Beliefs must be altered. Traditions must be reexamined, upholding those which are still appropriate and discarding those which are not. The "lewd, lusty language of the military conqueror" will have to give way to something less salty. A sexual joke will have to become as inappropriate as a racial slur. Demeaning and derogatory terms for women have to be eradicated, along with sexual innuendos and explicit requests for sexual encounters. It is time to reclaim the "refined manners, punctilious courtesy, and the nicest sense of personal honor" demanded by John Paul Jones. Those in authority must lead the way.

Sexual Harassment Is Overestimated

by Gretchen Morgenson

About the author: *Gretchen Morgenson is a senior editor for* Forbes, *a bimonthly financial and business magazine.*

On October 11, 1991, in the middle of the Anita Hill/Clarence Thomas contretemps, the *New York Times* somberly reported that sexual harassment pervades the American workplace. The source for this page-one story was a *Times*/CBS poll conducted two days earlier in which a handful (294) of women were interviewed by telephone. Thirty-eight per cent of respondents confirmed that they had been at one time or another "the object of sexual advances, propositions, or unwanted sexual discussions from men who supervise you or can affect your position at work." How many reported the incident at the time it happened? Four per cent.

Did the *Times* offer any explanation for why so few actually reported the incident? Could it be that these women did not report their "harassment" because they themselves did not regard a sexual advance as harassment? Some intelligent speculation on this matter might shed light on a key point: the vague definitions of harassment that make it easy to allege, hard to identify, and almost impossible to prosecute. Alas, the *Times* was in no mood to enlighten its readers.

Two Types of Harassment

It has been more than ten years since the Equal Employment Opportunity Commission (EEOC) wrote its guidelines defining sexual harassment as a form of sexual discrimination and, therefore, illegal under Title VII of the Civil Rights Act of 1964. According to the EEOC there are two different types of harassment: so-called *quid pro quo* harassment, in which career or job advancement is guaranteed in return for sexual favors, and environmental harassment, in which unwelcome sexual conduct "unreasonably interferes" with an individual's working environment or creates an "intimidating, hostile, or offensive working environment."

Following the EEOC's lead, an estimated three out of four companies nationwide have instituted strict policies against harassment; millions of dollars are spent each year educating employees in the subtleties of Title VII etiquette. Men are warned to watch their behavior, to jettison the patronizing pat and excise the sexist comment from their vocabularies.

"If you believe what you read in the newspapers, we are in the Stone Age where the sexes are concerned."

Yet, if you believe what you read in the newspapers, we are in the Stone Age where the sexes are concerned. A theme common to the media, plaintiff's lawyers, and employee-relations consultants is that male harassment of women is costing corporations millions each year in lost productivity and low employee morale. "Sexual harassment costs a typical Fortune 500 Service or Manufacturing company $6.7 million a year" says a sexual-harassment survey conducted late in 1988 for *Working Woman* by Klein Associates. This Boston consulting firm is part of a veritable growth industry which has sprung up to dispense sexual-harassment advice to worried companies in the form of seminars, videos, and encounter groups.

Hype and Hysteria

But is sexual harassment such a huge problem in business? Or is it largely a product of hype and hysteria? The statistics show that sexual harassment is less prevalent today than it was in 1986. According to the EEOC, federal cases alleging harassment on the job totaled 5,694 in 1990, compared to 6,342 in 1984. Yet today there are 17 per cent more women working than there were then.

At that, the EEOC's figures are almost certainly too high. In a good many of those complaints, sexual harassment may be tangential to the case; the complaint may primarily involve another form of discrimination in Title VII territory: race, national origin, or religious discrimination, for example. The EEOC doesn't separate cases involving sexual harassment alone; any case where sexual harassment is mentioned, even in passing, gets lumped into its figures.

Many of the stories depicting sexual harassment as a severe problem spring from "consultants" whose livelihoods depend upon exaggerating its extent. In one year, DuPont spent $450,000 on sexual-harassment training programs and materials. Susan Webb, president of Pacific Resources Development Group, a Seattle consultant, says she spends 95 per cent of her time advising on sexual harassment. Like most consultants, Miss Webb acts as an expert witness in harassment cases, conducts investigations for companies and municipalities, and teaches seminars. She charges clients $1,500 for her 35-minute sexual-harassment video program and handbooks.

47

Corporations began to express concern on the issue back in the early Eighties, just after the EEOC published its first guidelines. But it was *Meritor Savings Bank v. Vinson*, a harassment case that made it to the Supreme Court in 1985, that really acted as an employment act for sex-harassment consultants. In *Vinson*, the Court stated that employers could limit their liability to harassment claims by implementing anti-harassment policies and procedures in the workplace. And so, the anti-harassment industry was born.

Harassment Still a Problem

Naturally, the consultants believe they are filling a need, not creating one. "Harassment is still as big a problem as it has been because the workplace is not integrated," says Susan Webb. Ergo, dwindling numbers of cases filed with the EEOC are simply not indicative of a diminution in the problem.

Then what do the figures indicate? Two things, according to the harassment industry. First, that more plaintiffs are bringing private lawsuits against their employers than are suing through the EEOC or state civil-rights commissions. Second, that the number of cases filed is a drop in the bucket compared to the number of actual, everyday harassment incidents.

It certainly stands to reason that a plaintiff in a sexual-harassment case would prefer bringing a private action against her employer to filing an EEOC claim. EEOC and state civil-rights cases allow plaintiffs only compensatory damages, such as back pay or legal fees. In order to collect big money—punitive damages—from an employer, a plaintiff must file a private action.

> *"The number of private sexual-harassment cases launched today is greatly overstated."*

Yet there's simply no proof that huge or increasing numbers of private actions are being filed today. No data are collected on numbers of private harassment suits filed, largely because they're brought as tort actions—assault and battery, emotional distress, or breach of contract. During the second half of the Eighties, the San Francisco law firm of Orrick, Herrington, and Sutcliffe monitored private sexual-harassment cases filed in California. Its findings: From 1984 to 1989, the number of sexual-harassment cases in California that were litigated through to a verdict totaled a whopping 15. That's in a state with almost six million working women.

Of course, cases are often settled prior to a verdict. But how many? Orrick, Herrington partner Ralph H. Baxter Jr., management co-chairman of the American Bar Association's Labor Law Committee on Employee Rights and Responsibilities, believes the number of private sexual-harassment cases launched today is greatly overstated. "Litigation is not as big a problem as it's made out to be; you're not going to see case after case," says Mr. Baxter. "A high percentage of matters go to the EEOC and a substantial number of cases get resolved."

Those sexual-harassment actions that do get to a jury are the ones that really grab headlines. A couple of massive awards have been granted in recent years—five plaintiffs were awarded $3.8 million by a North Carolina jury—but most mammoth awards are reduced on appeal. In fact, million-dollar sexual-harassment verdicts are still exceedingly rare. In California, land of the happy litigator, the median jury verdict for all sexual-harassment cases litigated between 1984 and 1989 was $183,000. The top verdict in the state was just under $500,000, the lowest was $45,000. And California, known for its sympathetic jurors, probably produces higher awards than most states.

Now to argument number two: that the number of litigated harassment cases is tiny compared to the number of actual incidents that occur. Bringing a sexual-harassment case is similar to filing a rape case, consultants and lawyers say; both are nasty proceedings which involve defamation, possible job loss, and threats to both parties' family harmony.

Unfiled Cases

It may well be that cases of perceived harassment go unfiled, but is it reasonable to assume that the numbers of these unfiled cases run into the millions? Consider the numbers of cases filed that are dismissed for "no probable cause." According to the New York State human-rights commission, almost two-thirds of the complaints filed since 1986 were dismissed for lack of probable cause. Of the two hundred sexual-harassment cases the commission receives a year, 38 per cent bring benefits to the complainant.

What about private actions? No one keeps figures on the percentage of cases nationwide won by the plaintiff versus the percentage that are dismissed. However, the outcomes of private sexual-harassment suits brought in California from 1984 to 1989 mirror the public figures from New York. According to Orrick, Herrington, of the 15 cases litigated to a verdict in California from 1984 to 1989, slightly less than half were dismissed and slightly more than half (53 per cent) were won by the plaintiff.

Are California and New York anomalies? Stephen Perlman, a partner in labor law at the Boston firm of Ropes & Gray, who has 15 years' experience litigating sexual-harassment cases, thinks not: "I don't suppose I've had as many as a dozen cases go to litigation. Most of the cases I've seen—the vast majority—get dismissed. They don't even have probable cause to warrant further processing."

"A major problem is the vague definition of harassment."

A major problem is the vague definition of harassment. If "environmental harassment" were clearly defined and specifiable, lawyers would undoubtedly see more winnable cases walk through their doors. Asking a subordinate to perform sexual favors in exchange for a raise is clearly illegal. But a dirty joke? A pin-up? A request for a date?

In fact, behavior which one woman may consider harassment could be seen by another as a non-threatening joke. The closest thing to harassment that I have experienced during my 15-year career occurred in the early Eighties when I was a stockbroker-in-training at Dean Witter Reynolds in New York City. I had brought in the largest personal account within Dean Witter's entire retail brokerage system, an account

> *"Behavior which one woman may consider harassment could be seen by another as a non-threatening joke."*

which held roughly $20 million in blue-chip stocks. Having this account under my management meant I had a larger capital responsibility than any of my colleagues, yet I was relatively new to the business. My fellow brokers were curious, but only one was brutish enough to walk right up to me and pop the question: "How did you get that account? Did you sleep with the guy?"

Instead of running away in tears, I dealt with him as I would any rude person. "Yeah," I answered. "Eat your heart out." He turned on his heel and never bothered me again. Was my colleague a harasser, or just practicing Wall Street's aggressive humor, which is dished out to men in other ways? Apparently, I am in the minority in thinking the latter. But the question remains. Whose standards should be used to define harassment?

Under tort law, the behavior which has resulted in a case—such as an assault or the intent to cause emotional distress—must be considered objectionable by a "reasonable person." The EEOC follows this lead and in its guidelines defines environmental harassment as that which "unreasonably interferes with an individual's job performance."

Legislating Rude Behavior

Yet, sexual-harassment consultants argue that any such behavior—even that which is perceived as harassment only by the most hypersensitive employee—ought to be considered illegal and stamped out. In fact, they say, the subtler hostile-environment cases are the most common and cause the most anguish. Says Frieda Klein, the Boston consultant: "My goal is to create a corporate climate where every employee feels free to object to behavior, where people are clear about their boundaries and can ask that objectionable behavior stop."

Sounds great. But rudeness and annoying behavior cannot be legislated out of existence; nor should corporations be forced to live under the tyranny of a hypersensitive employee. No woman should have to run a daily gauntlet of sexual innuendo, but neither is it reasonable for women to expect a pristine work environment free of coarse behavior.

Susan Hartzoge Gray, a labor lawyer at Haworth, Riggs, Kuhn, and Haworth in Raleigh, North Carolina, believes that hostile-environment harassment shouldn't be actionable under Title VII. "How can the law say one person's lewd and another's nice?" she asks. "There are so many different taste levels. . . . We condone sexual jokes and innuendos in the media—a movie might get a PG rating—yet an employer can be called on the carpet because the same thing bothers someone in an office."

But changing demographics may do more to eliminate genuine sexual harassment than all the apparatus of law and consultancy. As women reach a critical mass in the workforce, the problem of sexual harassment tends to go away. Frieda Klein says the problem practically vanishes once 30 per cent of the workers in a department, an assembly line, or a company are women.

Reaching that critical mass won't take long. According to the Bureau of Labor Statistics, there will be 66 million women to 73 million men in the workplace by 2000. They won't all be running departments or heading companies, of course, but many will.

So sexual harassment will probably become even less of a problem in the years ahead than it is today. But you are not likely to read that story in a major newspaper anytime soon. Indeed, sexual harassment has all the earmarks of an issue Democrats will use to try to steal voters, particularly women, from the GOP. Such tactics are more likely to worsen the Democrats' already woeful standing with male voters, who went 58 per cent Republican in the last presidential election. The likelihood of losing more than they stand to gain from highlighting sexual harassment probably won't stop the Democrats—unless George Bush has saved them by endorsing the feminist agenda of punitive damages for vaguely defined sex-harassment charges in his new litigation-boosting civil-rights bill.

> *"Sexual harassment will probably become even less of a problem in the years ahead than it is today."*

51

Feminists Exaggerate the Seriousness of Sexual Harassment

by Naomi Munson

About the author: Writer Naomi Munson has contributed to many newspapers and periodicals, including the Wall Street Journal, *the* American Spectator, Contentions, *and* Commentary.

When I was graduated from college in the early '70s, I had the good fortune to land a job at a weekly newsmagazine. It was a wonderful place to work, financially lucrative, intellectually demanding but not overwhelming, and, above all, fun.

A Hierarchy of Fun

There was, actually, a sort of hierarchy of fun at the office. Ranking lowest were the hard-news departments; although (or perhaps because) they offered the excitement of late-breaking news and fast-developing stories, both the national- and the foreign-affairs sections were socially rather staid. Next up the scale came the business section, where the people were lively enough but where the general tone nevertheless reflected the serious nature of the subject matter. Then there was the culture department, a barrel of laughs in its own way, though the staff did seem to spend a certain amount of time at the opera. At the top of the scale stood the department where I wound up, which included science, sports, education, religion, and the like. Though there might be the occasional breaking news, these sections generally called more for long thought and thorough research, which led to a very laid-back atmosphere and a lot of down time. Drinking at nearby bars, dining at the finest restaurants, and dancing at local discos occupied a great deal of that time. And sex played a major role in all of this. (It did throughout the magazine, of course, but nowhere so openly and unselfconsciously as here.)

The men were a randy lot, dedicated philanderers, and foulmouthed to boot; the women, having vociferously demanded—and been granted—absolutely equal status, were considered fair game (though there were a couple of secretaries whose advancing age and delicate sensibilities consigned them to the sidelines).

Imagine my surprise, then, when one day a young woman who worked with me flounced into my office, cheeks flushed, eyes flashing, to announce that she had just been sub-

> *"The charge of sexual harassment would serve as a perfect instrument of revenge for disgruntled female employees."*

jected to sexual harassment. (It was a fairly new concept back then, at the end of the '70s, but being in the vanguard of social trends, we had heard of it.) When she explained that the offense had occurred not in our own neck of the woods but in the national affairs section, I was truly shocked. When she identified the offender, however—sexually, one of the least lively types on the premises—I began to be skeptical. And when she described his crime—which was having said something to the effect that he longed for the good old days of miniskirts when a fellow had a real chance to see great legs like hers—I scoffed. "Oh, come on," I said. "That's not sexual harassment; that's just D. trying to pay you a compliment." To myself, after she had calmed down and left, I said, "She's even dimmer than I thought. She thinks *that's* what they mean by sexual harassment."

If I was convinced that this woman's experience did not constitute sexual harassment, I, like the vast majority of people at that time, had rather vague notions of what did. Whatever it was, however, it already seemed clear that the charge of sexual harassment would serve as a perfect instrument of revenge for disgruntled female employees. This was borne out by the story I came to know, years later, about a man at another office who had had several formal harassment charges brought against him by women who worked for him. The man was someone who would, as his coworkers saw it, "nail" anything that moved. He had, in fact, had longstanding affairs—which he had ended in order to move on to fresh conquests—with the women now accusing him of having offered financial inducements in exchange for sexual favors. The women claimed to have declined the offers and consequently suffered the loss of promotions.

Sex and Sexual Harassment

Disgruntlement aside, however, it still seemed obvious to me that in a case of sexual harassment, something *sexual* might be supposed to have occurred. That quaint notion of mine was finally laid to rest during the Clarence Thomas-Anita Hill debacle. Professor Hill's performance convinced me of nothing save that if she told me the sun was shining, I should head straight for my umbrella and ga-loshes. The vast outpouring of feminist outrage that accompanied the event did, however, succeed in opening my eyes to the sad fact that it was I, way back when, who had been the dim one; my erstwhile colleague had merely been a bit ahead of her time. For, it now turns out, what she described is precisely what they *do* mean by sexual harassment.

During the course of the hearing, story after story appeared in the media sup-porting the claim that men out there are abusive to their female employees. It was declared, over and over, that virtually every woman in the country had ei-ther suffered sexual harassment herself or knew someone who had (I myself, I realize, figure in that assessment). The abuse, it appeared, had been going on since time immemorial and was so painful to some of the women involved that they had repressed it for decades.

It became clear amid all the hand-wringing that we were not talking here about bosses exacting sexual favors in exchange for promotions, raises, or the like. Even Professor Hill never claimed that Judge Thomas promised to promote her if she succumbed to his charms, or that he threatened to fire her if she failed to do so. What she said, as all the world now knows, was that he pestered her for dates; that he boasted of his natu-ral endowments and of his sexual prowess; that he used obscene lan-guage in her presence; that he regaled her with the details of porno flicks;

> *"Single women were heard to worry that putting a lid on sex at the office might hurt their chances of finding a husband."*

and that he discussed the joys of, as Miss Hill so expressively put it, "(gulp) oral sex." The closest anyone at the hearing came to revealing anything like direct action was a Washington woman who was horrified when a member of Congress played footsie with her under the table at an official function, and a friend of Anita Hill who announced that she had been "touched in the workplace."

Unpleasantness and Insensitivity

What we—or, to be more precise, they—were talking about was sexual innu-endo, ogling, obscenity, unwelcome importuning, nude pin-ups; about an "un-pleasant atmosphere in the workplace"; about male "insensitivity." One colum-nist offered behavioral guidelines to men who had been reduced to "whining" that they no longer knew what was appropriate—something to the effect that though it is OK to say, "Gee, I bet you make the best blackened redfish in town," it is not OK to say, "Wow, I bet you're really hot between the sheets." Even Judge Thomas himself declared that if he *had* said the things the good professor was accusing him of, it *would* have constituted sexual harassment.

Yet in response to all of this it also emerged very plainly that the American public just was not buying it. Single women were heard to worry that putting a lid on sex at the office might hurt their chances of finding a husband; one forthright woman was even quoted by a newspaper as saying that office sex was the spice of life. Rather more definitively, polls showed that most people, black and white, male and female, thought Judge Thomas should be confirmed, *even if the charges against him were true.*

> **"Women have always managed to deal perfectly well with male lust: to evade it, to quash it, even to be flattered by it."**

How can it be that the majority of Americans were dismissing the significance of sexual harassment (as now defined) even as their elected representatives were declaring it just the most hideous, heinous, gosh-awful stuff they had ever heard of? How is it possible that, at the very moment newspapers and TV were proclaiming that American women were mad as hell and weren't going to take it anymore, most of these women themselves—and their husbands—were responding with a raised eyebrow and a small shrug of the shoulders?

For one thing, most Americans—unlike the ideologues who brought us sexual harassment in the first place, and who have worked a special magic on pundits and politicos for more than two decades now—have a keen understanding of life's realities. Having had no choice but to work, in order to feed and clothe and doctor and educate their children, they have always known that, while work has its rewards, financial and otherwise, "an unpleasant atmosphere in the workplace" is something they may well have to put up with. That, where women are concerned, the unpleasantness might take on sexual overtones gives it no more weight than the uncertainties, the frustrations, and the humiliations, petty and grand, encountered by men.

Most people, furthermore, have a healthy respect for the ability of women to hold their own in the battle of the sexes. They know that women have always managed to deal perfectly well with male lust: to evade it, to quash it, even to be flattered by it. The bepaunched and puffing boss, chasing his buxom secretary around the desk, is, after all, a figure of fun—because we realize that he will never catch her, and that even if he did, she would know very well how to put him in his place.

The women's movement and its fellow travelers, on the other hand, have never had any such understanding or any such respect. On the contrary, rage against life's imperfections, and a consequent revulsion against men, has been the bone and sinew of that movement.

A History of Feminism

The feminists came barreling into the work force, some twenty years ago, not out of necessity, but with the loud assertion that here was to be found something called fulfillment. Men, they claimed, had denied them access to this fulfillment out of sheer power-hungry selfishness. Women, they insisted, were no different from men in their talents or their dispositions; any apparent differences had simply been manufactured, as a device to deprive mothers, wives, and sisters of the excitement and pleasure to which men had had exclusive title for so long, and which they had come to view as their sole privilege.

No sooner had these liberated ladies taken their rightful place alongside men at work, however, than it began to dawn on them that the experience was not quite living up to their expectations. They quickly discovered, for example, what their fathers, husbands, and brothers had always known: that talent is not always appreciated, that promotions are not so easy to come by, that often those most meritorious are inexplicably passed over in favor of others. But rather than recognizing this as a universal experience, they descried a "glass ceiling," especially constructed to keep them in their place, and they called for the hammers.

Feminists and Childbearing

Feminists had insisted that childbearing held no more allure for them than it did for men. That insistence quickly began to crumble in the face of a passionate desire for babies. But rather than recognizing that life had presented them with a choice, they demanded special treatment. They reserved the right to take leave from their work each time the urge to procreate came upon them. And they insisted that husbands, employers, and even the government take equal responsibility with them for the care and upbringing of the little bundles of joy resulting from that urge.

And as for sex in the workplace, well, that was pretty much what it had always been everywhere: an ongoing battle involving, on the one side, attentions both unwelcome and welcome, propositions both unappealing and appealing, and compliments both unpleasing and pleasing, and on the other, evasive action, outright rejection, or happy capitulation. Having long ago decided that the terms of this age-old battle were unacceptable to them, the women of the movement might have been expected to try to eliminate them. With the invention of sexual harassment, they have met that expectation, and with a vengeance. Laws have been made, cases have been tried and, in the Clarence Thomas affair, a decent man was pilloried.

Having, in other words, finally been permitted to play with the big boys, these women have found the game not to their liking. But rather than retiring from the field, they have called for a continuous and open-ended reformation of the rules. Indeed, like children in a temper, who respond to maternal placating with a rise in fury, they have met every accommodating act of the men in their lives with a further escalation of demand. The new insistence that traditional male expressions of sexual interest be declared taboo, besides being the purest revelation of feminist rage, is the latest arc in that vicious cycle.

Exaggerating the Extent of Sexual Harassment Harms Women

by Ellen Frankel Paul

About the author: *Ellen Frankel Paul is a political science professor and deputy director of the Social Philosophy and Policy Center at Bowling Green State University in Ohio. She is the author of* Equity and Gender: The Comparable Worth Debate *and* Property Rights and Eminent Domain.

Women in American society are victims of sexual harassment in alarming proportions. Sexual harassment is an inevitable corollary to class exploitation; as capitalists exploit workers, so do males in positions of authority exploit their female subordinates. Male professors, supervisors, and apartment managers in ever increasing numbers take advantage of the financial dependence and vulnerability of women to extract sexual concessions.

Valid Assertions?

These are the assertions that commonly begin discussions of sexual harassment. For reasons that will be adumbrated below, dissent from the prevailing view is long overdue. Three recent episodes will serve to frame this disagreement.

Valerie Craig, an employee of Y & Y Snacks, Inc., joined several co-workers and her supervisor for drinks after work one day in July of 1978. Her supervisor drove her home and proposed that they become more intimately acquainted. She refused his invitation for sexual relations, whereupon he said that he would "get even" with her. Ten days after the incident she was fired from her job. She soon filed a complaint of sexual harassment with the Equal Employment Opportunity Commission (EEOC), and the case wound its way through the courts. Craig prevailed, the company was held liable for damages, and she received back pay, reinstatement, and an order prohibiting Y & Y from taking reprisals against her in the future.

Carol Zabowicz, one of only two female forklift operators in a West Bend Co. warehouse, charged that her co-workers over a four year period from 1978–1982 sexually harassed her by such acts as: asking her whether she was wearing a bra; two of the men exposing their buttocks between ten and twenty times; a male co-worker grabbing his crotch and making obscene suggestions or growling; subjecting her to offensive and abusive language; and exhibiting obscene drawings with her initials on them. Zabowicz began to show symptoms of physical and psychological stress, necessitating several medical leaves, and she filed a sexual harassment complaint with the EEOC. The district court judge remarked that "the sustained, malicious, and brutal harassment meted out . . . was more than merely unreasonable; it was malevolent and outrageous." The company knew of the harassment and took corrective action only after the employee filed a complaint with the EEOC. The company was, therefore, held liable, and Zabowicz was awarded back pay for the period of her medical absence, and a judgment that her rights were violated under the Civil Rights Act of 1964.

> *"For women to expect reverential treatment in the workplace is utopian."*

On September 17, 1990, Lisa Olson, a sports reporter for the *Boston Herald*, charged five football players of the just-defeated New England Patriots with sexual harassment for making sexually suggestive and offensive remarks to her when she entered their locker room to conduct a post-game interview. The incident amounted to nothing short of "mind rape," according to Olson. After vociferous lamentations in the media, the National Football League fined the team and its players $25,000 each. The National Organization of Women called for a boycott of Remington electric shavers because the owner of the company, Victor Kiam, also owns the Patriots and who allegedly displayed insufficient sensitivity at the time when the episode occurred.

Utopian Treatment for Women

All these incidents are indisputably disturbing. In an ideal world—one needless to say far different from the one that we inhabit or are ever likely to inhabit—women would not be subjected to such treatment in the course of their work. Women, and men as well, would be accorded respect by co-workers and supervisors, their feelings would be taken into account, and their dignity would be left intact. For women to expect reverential treatment in the workplace is utopian, yet they should not have to tolerate outrageous, offensive sexual overtures and threats as they go about earning a living.

One question that needs to be pondered is: What kinds of undesired sexual behavior women should be protected against by law? That is, what kind of actions are deemed so outrageous and violate a woman's rights to such extent that the law should intervene, and what actions should be considered inconveniences of life, to be morally condemned but not adjudicated? A subsidiary question concerns the type of legal remedy appropriate for the wrongs that do require redress. Before directly addressing these questions, it might be useful to diffuse some of the hyperbole adhering to the sexual harassment issue.

Harassment Surveys

Surveys are one source of this hyperbole. If their results are accepted at face value, they lead to the conclusion that women are disproportionately victims of legions of sexual harassers. A poll by the Albuquerque *Tribune* found that nearly 80 percent of the respondents reported that they or someone they knew had been victims of sexual harassment. The Merit Systems Protection Board determined that 42 percent of the women (and 14 percent of men) working for the federal government had experienced some form of unwanted sexual attention between 1985 and 1987, with unwanted "sexual teasing" identified as the most prevalent form. A Defense Department survey found that 64 percent of women in the military (and 17 percent of the men) suffered "uninvited and unwanted sexual attention" within the previous year. The United Methodist Church established that 77 percent of its clergywomen experienced incidents of sexual harassment, with 41 percent of these naming a pastor or colleague as the perpetrator, and 31 percent mentioning church social functions as the setting.

> *"Sexual harassment is a notoriously ill-defined and almost infinitely expandable concept."*

A few caveats concerning polls in general, and these sorts of polls in particular, are worth considering. Pollsters looking for a particular social ill tend to find it, usually in gargantuan proportions. (What fate would lie in store for a pollster who concluded that child abuse, or wife beating, or mistreatment of the elderly had dwindled to the point of negligibility!) Sexual harassment is a notoriously ill-defined and almost infinitely expandable concept, including everything from rape to unwelcome neck massaging, discomfiture upon witnessing sexual overtures directed at others, yelling at and blowing smoke in the ears of female subordinates, and displays of pornographic pictures in the workplace. Defining sexual harassment, as the United Methodists did, as "any sexually related behavior that is unwelcome, offensive or which fails to respect the rights of others," the concept is broad enough to include everything from "unsolicited suggestive looks or leers [or] pressures for dates" to "actual sexual assaults or rapes." Categorizing everything from rape to "looks" as sexual harassment makes us all victims, a state of affairs satisfying to radical feminists, but not very useful for distinguishing serious injuries from the merely trivial.

Yet, even if the surveys exaggerate the extent of sexual harassment, however defined, what they do reflect is a great deal of tension between the sexes. As women in ever increasing numbers entered the workplace in the last two decades, as the women's movement challenged alleged male hegemony and exploitation with ever greater intemperance, and as women entered previously all-male preserves from the board rooms to the coal pits, it is lamentable, but should not be surprising, that this tension sometimes takes sexual form. Not that sexual harassment on the job, in the university, and in other settings is a trivial or insignificant matter, but a sense of proportion needs to be restored and, even

> *"Catagorizing everything from rape to 'looks' as sexual harassment makes us all victims."*

more importantly, distinctions need to be made. In other words, sexual harassment must be de-ideologized. Statements that paint nearly all women as victims and all men and their patriarchal, capitalist system as perpetrators, are ideological fantasy. Ideology blurs the distinction between being injured—being a genuine victim—and merely being offended. An example is this statement by Catharine A. MacKinnon, a law professor and feminist activist:

> Sexual harassment perpetuates the interlocked structure by which women have been kept sexually in thrall to men and at the bottom of the labor market. Two forces of American society converge: men's control over women's sexuality and capital's control over employees' work lives. Women historically have been required to exchange sexual services for material survival, in one form or another. Prostitution and marriage as well as sexual harassment in different ways institutionalize this arrangement.

Such hyperbole needs to be diffused and distinctions need to be drawn. Rape, a nonconsensual invasion of a person's body, is a crime clear and simple. It is a violation of the right to the physical integrity of the body (the right to life, as John Locke or Thomas Jefferson would have put it). Criminal law should and does prohibit rape. Whether it is useful to call rape "sexual harassment" is doubtful, for it makes the latter concept overly broad while trivializing the former.

Extortion of Sexual Favors

Intimidation in the workplace of the kind that befell Valerie Craig—that is, extortion of sexual favors by a supervisor from a subordinate by threatening to penalize, fire, or fail to reward—is what the courts term *quid pro quo* sexual harassment. Since the mid-1970s, the federal courts have treated this type of sexual harassment as a form of sex discrimination in employment proscribed under Title VII of the Civil Rights Act of 1964. A plaintiff who prevails against an employer may receive such equitable remedies as reinstatement and back pay, and the court can order the company to prepare and disseminate a policy against sexual harassment. Current law places principal liability on the company, not the harassing supervisor, even when higher management is unaware of the harassment and, thus, cannot take any steps to prevent it.

Quid pro quo sexual harassment is morally objectionable and analogous to extortion: The harasser extorts property (i.e., use of the woman's body) through the leverage of fear for her job. The victim of such behavior should have legal recourse, but serious reservations can be held about rectifying these injustices through the blunt instrument of Title VII. In egregious cases the victim is left less than whole (for back pay will not compensate her for ancillary losses), and no prospect for punitive damages are offered to deter would-be harassers. Even more distressing about Title VII is the fact that the primary target of litigation is not the actual harasser, but rather the employer. This places a double burden on a company. The employer is swindled by the supervisor because he spent his time pursuing sexual gratification and thereby impairing the efficiency of the workplace by mismanaging his subordinates, and the employer must endure lengthy and expensive litigation, pay damages, and suffer loss to its reputation. It would be fairer to both the company and the victim to treat sexual harassment as a tort—that is, as a private wrong or injury for which the court can assess damages. Employers should be held vicariously liable only when they know of an employee's behavior and do not try to redress it.

> *"Statements that paint nearly all women as victims and all men . . . as perpetrators, are ideological fantasy."*

Defining Harassment Is Difficult

As for the workplace harassment endured by Carol Zabowicz—the bared buttocks, obscene portraits, etc.—that too should be legally redressable. Presently, such incidents also fall under the umbrella of Title VII, and are termed hostile environment sexual harassment, a category accepted later than *quid pro quo* and with some judicial reluctance. The main problem with this category is that it has proven too elastic: cases have reached the courts based on everything from off-color jokes to unwanted, persistent sexual advances by co-workers. A new tort of sexual harassment would handle these cases better. Only instances above a certain threshold of egregiousness or outrageousness would be actionable. In other words, the behavior that the plaintiff found offensive would also have to be offensive to the proverbial "reasonable man" of the tort law. That is, the behavior would have to be objectively injurious rather than merely subjectively offensive. The defendant would be the actual harasser, not the company, unless it knew about the problem and failed to act. Victims of scatological jokes, leers, unwanted offers of dates, and other sexual annoyances would no longer have their day in court.

A distinction must be restored between morally offensive behavior and behavior that causes serious harm. Only the latter should fall under the jurisdiction of criminal or tort law. Do we really want legislators and judges delving into our most intimate private lives, deciding when a look is a leer, and when a leer is a Civil Rights Act offense? Do we really want courts deciding, as one recently did, whether a school principal's disparaging remarks about a female school district administrator was sexual harassment and, hence, a breach of Title VII, or merely the act of a spurned and vengeful lover? Do we want judges settling disputes such as the one that arose at a car dealership after a female employee turned down a male co-worker's offer of a date and his colleagues retaliated by calling her offensive names and embarrassing her in front of customers? Or another case in which a female shipyard worker complained of an "offensive working environment" because of the prevalence of pornographic material on the docks? Do we want the state to prevent or compensate us for any behavior that someone might find offensive? Should people have a legally enforceable right not to be offended by others? At some point, the price for such protection is the loss of both liberty and privacy rights.

No Perfect Working Environment Exists

Workplaces are breeding grounds of envy, personal grudges, infatuation, and jilted loves, and beneath a fairly high threshold of outrageousness, these travails should be either suffered in silence, complained of to higher management, or left behind as one seeks other employment. No one, female or male, can expect to enjoy a working environment that is perfectly stress-free, or to be treated always and by everyone with kindness and respect. To the extent that sympathetic judges have encouraged women to seek monetary compensation for slights and annoyances, they have not done them a great service. Women need to develop a thick skin in order to survive and prosper in the workforce. It is patronizing to think that they need to be recompensed by male judges for seeing a few pornographic pictures on a wall. By their efforts to extend sexual harassment charges to even the most trivial behavior, the radical feminists send a message that women are not resilient enough to ignore the run-of-the-mill, churlish provocation from male co-workers. It is difficult to imagine a suit by a longshoreman complaining of mental stress due to the display of nude male centerfolds by female co-workers.

> **"Quid pro quo *sexual harassment is morally objectionable and analogous to extortion."***

Women cannot expect to have it both ways: equality where convenient, but special dispensations when the going gets rough. Equality has its price and that price may include unwelcome sexual advances, irritating and even intimidating sexual jests, and lewd and obnoxious colleagues.

Egregious acts—sexual harassment per se—must be legally redressable. Lesser but not trivial offenses, whether at the workplace or in other more social settings, should be considered moral lapses for which the offending party receives opprobrium, disciplinary warnings, or penalties, depending on the setting and the severity. Trivial offenses, dirty jokes, sexual overtures, and sexual innuendoes do make many women feel intensely discomfited, but, unless they become outrageous through persistence or content, these too should be taken as part of life's annoyances. The perpetrators should be either endured, ignored, rebuked, or avoided, as circumstances and personal inclination dictate. Whether Lisa Olson's experience in the locker room of the Boston Patriots falls into the second or third category is debatable. The media circus triggered by the incident was certainly out of proportion to the event.

As the presence of women on road gangs, construction crews, and oil rigs becomes a fact of life, the animosities and tensions of this transition period are likely to abate gradually. Meanwhile, women should "lighten up," and even dispense a few risqué barbs of their own, a sure way of taking the fun out of it for offensive male bores.

Chapter 2

What Causes
Sexual Harassment?

CURRENT CONTROVERSIES

Chapter Preface

According to sexual harassment studies completed since 1987, there is no stereotypical harasser. Although sexual harassers are more likely to be men than women, they can come from any profession, age group, or race. What causes harassers to abuse the people they come into contact with, especially in a work environment? The explanations offered for this seemingly random pattern of harassment can be separated into two general types. The first type identifies sexual harassment as a symptom of large moral or political trends in society, such as the sexual revolution. The second type identifies narrower causes, such as pornography.

Many of those experts who believe sexual harassment is caused by broad societal problems point to the loosening of sexual morals that accompanied the sexual revolution. They say this change in the moral climate makes sexual comments and advances more socially acceptable. Others believe the power hierarchies of capitalism place people in a competitive environment, encouraging them to control and dominate their coworkers. Sexual harassment is one form of such control. Those who believe in broad causes say the problem of sexual harassment can only be solved by addressing widespread societal problems.

Other researchers, however, believe that specific societal problems directly cause people to sexually harass others. One example is pornography, which some people feel objectifies women, reducing men's respect for them. They believe the widespread availability of pornography explains why so many different types of people become harassers. Some researchers argue that if society reduced the supply of pornography, it could reduce the incidence of sexual harassment. Another narrow explanation for sexual harassment is the confusing legislation and court decisions that have made it difficult for women to effectively prosecute sexual harassment cases. Some researchers argue that a simpler, more consistent legal system would reduce sexual harassment because the penalties that would result from successful prosecutions would discourage further harassment.

Many experts believe that correctly identifying the cause of sexual harassment is the key to preventing it. If there are widespread social causes of the problem, then education or general reform movements such as feminism may eradicate sexual harassment. However, if there is one element in society that is causing people to become harassers, then legislation to eliminate that influence could remedy the problem. The viewpoints in this chapter discuss possible causes of sexual harassment, presenting both broad, societal explanations and narrow, direct theories.

Men's Insecurity Causes Sexual Harassment

by Daniel Goleman

About the author: *Daniel Goleman is a reporter for the* New York Times.

Consider the case of a male supervisor who, in the midst of a conversation with a female employee about an assignment, asked her out of the blue, "Are you wearing panties?" and then blithely continued the conversation seemingly pleased that he had left her rattled. Years later, the woman says she is still outraged by the incident, though she said nothing at the time. One of a flood of tales that have surfaced in the wake of Anita F. Hill's accusations of sexual harassment in hearings on Clarence Thomas's Supreme Court nomination, the story underscores a picture that is emerging from extensive research on such harassment: it has less to do with sex than with power. It is a way to keep women in their place; through harassment men devalue a woman's role in the work place by calling attention to her sexuality.

"Sexual harassment is a subtle rape, and rape is more about fear than sex," said Dr. John Gottman, a psychologist at the University of Washington. "Harassment is a way for a man to make a woman vulnerable."

While sexual harassment may on first glance be taken as simple social ineptness or as an awkward expression of romantic attraction, researchers say that view is wrong and pernicious because it can lead women who suffer harassment to blame themselves, believing that something in their dress or behavior might have brought the unwanted attention.

Harassment Not Seduction

In fact, only about 25 percent of cases of sexual harassment are botched seductions, in which the man "is trying to get someone into bed," said Dr. Louise Fitzgerald, a psychologist at the University of Illinois. "And in less than 5 percent of cases the harassment involves a bribe or threat for sex, where the man is saying, 'If you do this for me, I'll help you at work, and if you don't, I'll make things difficult for you.'" The rest, she said, are assertions of power.

The use of harassment as a tactic to control or frighten women, researchers say, explains why sexual harassment is most frequent in occupations and work places where women are new and are in the minority. In fact, no matter how many men they encounter in the course of their work, women who hold jobs traditionally held by men are far more likely to be harassed than women who do "women's work."

For example, a 1989 study of 100 women working in a factory found that those who were machinists, not a

> *"Sexual harassment is a subtle rape, . . . a way for a man to make a woman vulnerable."*

job traditionally held by women, reported being harassed far more than those on the assembly line, where more women work. Women in both groups encountered about the same number of men at work.

"On all 28 items of a sexual harassment scale, ranging from lewd remarks to sexual assault, the women machinists had the highest scores," said Dr. Nancy Baker, a psychologist in Los Angeles who conducted the study. "Among women in white-collar jobs, the same holds true. The more nontraditional the job for women, the more sexual harassment. Women surgeons and investment bankers rank among the highest for harassment."

The style of harassment also is likely to differ among professionals and blue-collar workers. "In the blue-collar work place there's often a real hostility to women," said Dr. Fitzgerald. "Men see women as invading a masculine environment. These are guys whose sexual harassment has nothing whatever to do with sex. They're trying to scare women off a male preserve."

Dr. Fitzgerald added, "Professional men don't go around putting used condoms in your desk, as can happen in a blue-collar setting. It's more likely to be something like what happened to a woman lawyer I know at a large international firm. As she was sitting at a conference table with other executives, all men, she said, 'I have two points,' and one of the men interrupted, 'Yes you do, and they look wonderful.'"

Generation Gap

Some harassment simply seems to result from what Dr. Fitzgerald calls a "cultural lag." "Many men entered the work place at a time when sexual teasing and innuendo were commonplace," she said. "They have no sense there's anything wrong with it. All they need is some education."

But genuine harassers, Dr. Fitzgerald said, "continue to do offensive things even when a woman tells them it is obnoxious."

In a 1981 study of 10,648 women working for the Federal Government, 42 percent said they had been harassed. In a third of cases the harassment took the form of unwanted sexual remarks; 28 percent involved leers and suggestive looks, and a quarter involved being touched. About 15 percent of women complained of being pressured for dates, and 9 percent said they had been pressured for sexual favors. One percent reported being assaulted or raped at work.

Sexual harassment of men is much less common and is little studied by researchers.

Differing Perceptions

To be sure, there is a gulf in men's and women's perceptions, a gray zone that may itself lead to some instances of harassment. For instance, in a random telephone survey of 1,000 men and women in Los Angeles, Dr. Barbara Gutek, a psychologist at the University of Arizona business school, found that 67 percent of men said they would be complimented if they were propositioned by a woman at work. Seventeen percent of women said so. The same survey found that 10 percent of women had left a job because of sexual harassment.

Perhaps the most startling finding on the gulf between men and women in awareness about sexual harassment came in a study by Dr. Michelle Paludi, a psychologist at Hunter College who coordinates a committee there on sexual harassment. In the study, men and women in college were presented with hypothetical scenarios and asked to say when sexual harassment occurred.

In one scenario, a woman gets a job teaching at a university and her department chairman, a man, invites her to lunch to discuss her research. At lunch he never mentions her research, but instead delves into her personal life. After a few such lunches he invites her to dinner and then for drinks. While they are having drinks, he tries to fondle her.

"Most of the women said that sexual harassment started at the first lunch, when he talked about her private life instead of her work," said Dr. Paludi. "Most of the men said that sexual harassment began at the point he fondled her."

Dr. Paludi added, "There is a difference between intent and impact. Many may not intend it, but some things they do may be experienced by women as sexual harassment. A touch or comment can be seen very differently."

> *"Sexual harassment has nothing whatever to do with sex. They're trying to scare women off a male preserve."*

While the current uproar about sexual harassment may make some men feel uneasy that some of their own behavior could be construed by women as sexual harassment, the best guess is that fewer than 1 percent of men are chronic harassers, said Dr. Gutek.

Until the confirmation hearings for Judge Thomas, "sexual harassment was the last great open secret," said Dr. Fitzgerald, who was scheduled to appear as an expert witness but was not called. "Although most women have known about it, and most will experience it at some point, until recently it did not even have a name—a fact that contributed to its continuation," she said.

The term "sexual harassment" was first used in a legal case in 1976 and did not come into wide popular use until the mid-1980s.

In research with 832 working women, Dr. Gutek found that although nearly half said they had been sexually harassed, none had sought legal recourse, and only 22 percent said they had told anyone else about the incident.

Several studies have found that only 3 percent of women who have been sexually harassed make a formal complaint. "We find that close to 90 percent of women who have been sexually harassed want to leave but can't because they need their job," said Dr. Paludi.

Despite company policies forbidding harassment, many victims say they believe that reporting it will simply lead to more trouble. In a study of 2,000 women working at large state universities, Dr. Fitzgerald found that most had not reported sexual harassment because they feared they would not be believed, that they would suffer retaliation, would be labeled as troublemakers, or would lose their jobs. Some women say they stay silent because they fear that reporting an incident may cost the harasser his job or his marriage.

> *"Some women say they stay silent because they fear that reporting an incident may cost the harasser his job or his marriage."*

Another reason most women who are sexually harassed remain silent is that "women feel a responsibility to be emotional managers of relationships and often want to keep things friendly," said Antonio Abbey, a psychologist at Wayne State University.

In research with victims of sexual harassment, Dr. Paludi has found that the emotional aftermath can be similar to that found in victims of traumas like rape or assault.

Capitalism Causes Sexual Harassment

by Li Onesto

About the author: *Li Onesto is a frequent contributor to the* Revolutionary Worker, *the weekly newspaper of the Revolutionary Communist party.*

"In the workplace, sexual harassment fixes the low status of women irreversibly. Women are sex; even filing or typing, women are sex. The debilitating, insidious violence of sexual harassment is pervasive in the workplace. It is part of nearly every working environment. Women shuffle; women placate; women submit; women leave; the rare, brave women fight and are tied up in the courts, often without jobs, for years. There is also rape in the workplace.

"Where is the place for intelligence—for literacy, intellect, creativity, moral discernment? Where in this world in which women live, circumscribed by the uses to which men put women's sexual organs, is the cultivation of skills, the cultivation of gifts, the cultivation of dreams, the cultivation of ambition?"

Andrea Dworkin in *Right Wing Women*

Polls and surveys reveal an ugly situation: 40 to 70 percent of all working women have experienced some form of sexual harassment on the job. In a *New York Times*/CBS News poll, four out of ten women said they encountered what they regarded as sexual harassment at work. Five out of ten men said that at some point on the job, they had said or done something that could have been construed as sexual harassment. And 38 percent of the women said they had found themselves the "object of sexual advances, propositions or unwanted sexual discussions" from men who supervise them or could affect their position at work. Only one out of ten of the women who were sexually harassed felt the freedom to report the incidents.

Sexual harassment is clearly a huge problem in this society. More then 58

Li Onesto, "Sexual Harassment: It's a Bourgeois Thang," *Revolutionary Worker*, November 3, 1991. Reprinted with permission of the *Revolutionary Worker*, the weekly newspaper of the Revolutionary Communist Party, U.S.A. The title of this viewpoint and the subheadings have been inserted by Greenhaven Press.

million women work in the U.S. making up more than 45 percent of the total workforce. And a very large percentage of these women, on a day-to-day basis, face conditions that are demeaning, humiliating and threatening *because of their sex.*

[Lately,] millions of people have been talking about the issue of sexual harassment. Many women have stepped forward to speak bitterness about their personal experiences and the pervasiveness of sexual harassment. There is a lot of anger and rage. And there has been widespread debate and discussion. Clearly, this issue has touched a deep nerve in society.

> *"38 percent of the women said they had found themselves the 'object of sexual advances, propositions or unwanted sexual discussions.'"*

Anyone who is for the liberation of women—and getting rid of all forms of oppression—needs to get clear on what sexual harassment is, what it reveals about this system, and what it's going to take to deal with this problem.

Power Relations

There is a lot of talk about how, when it comes to sexual harassment, men "just don't get it." Some men and even some women say, "what's the big deal"—can't women take a joke? There's a backlash from some men who complain that now, after all this public debate, men who are just "awkward" about asking for a date will be unjustly accused. Former editor of *Newsweek* William Broyles Jr. claimed in the *New York Times* that "the rules of sexual harassment are not objective" and that "each woman makes her own law." He whines, "If a man wants to ask a co-worker out, he shouldn't have to bring his lawyer along."

But all this talk misses the point—or more consciously tries to cover up—what sexual harassment is really all about. It is quite an exposure in itself that here we have millions of women who face an abusive and humiliating situation in the workplace and the first response of many men is that they are worried about how all this talk of sexual harassment will put a "cramp" on their ability to ask women out for a date! This just goes to show how deep male privilege and chauvinist attitudes are in this society.

But more to the point is the fact that relations between men and women in this society—from top to bottom, and whether you're talking about dating or on-the-job interaction between men and women—are FILLED with power trips and oppressive relations where women are subordinated and abused *as women.* The objectification of women, the "hunting" attitudes of men, and the general treatment of women as inferior human beings whose role in society is to serve husband and children—all this is promoted and upheld from the highest offices of government. All this is socially taught to men from the time they are young boys and it's constantly offered up as justification for petty male privileges. So

71

if all this talk about sexual harassment is helping to get these kinds of things out in the open, and if women calling this out is "putting a cramp" on some such attitudes and practices towards women, then that's a very good thing!

But let's look at the phenomenon of sexual harassment on another level. The overall relations between men and women in society are bound to exert a powerful force in work situations where women and men are working together. Sexual relations generally in society are stamped with *power* relations, and sexual harassment is about the exercise of *power* by men over women. While it may be carried out by *individual* men, it is one way that male domination is enforced in society overall. It is part of an oppressive political program for women that is promoted more broadly in society.

Women know well the ways sexual harassment takes place: from jokes and comments meant to humiliate you to daily comments about your appearance. There's the subtle—or explicit—threat that you could be fired if you don't respond to various sexual come-ons. And there's the insulting promise that you'll be promoted if you date the boss. These experiences bring together two ugly features of the bourgeois way of life: the general oppressive way women are treated and sexually objectified by men in this society and the oppressive relations of production under capitalism more generally.

The Power Trips of Capitalism

Sexual harassment on the job is a particular way that dog-eat-dog competition under capitalism gets expressed. It takes different forms among different classes. But from the corporate office to the factory floor, there are the power trips, the back-stabbing, and rumor mongering that are all part of "getting ahead on the job."

Capitalism is based on private property and the exploitation of labor. And it produces economic and social relationships that viciously pit people against each other. We're told that competition is "healthy," provides incentive and is a necessary part of progress. But in real life it means a whole bureaucratic hierarchy of oppressive relationships where people are told that the only way to get ahead is by stepping on others. This is not a system that promotes cooperation and mutual respect. This is a system that promotes dog-eat-dog competition and thrives

> *"Relations between men and women . . . are FILLED with power trips and oppressive relations."*

on male domination and national oppression. This system produces *bourgeois relations* which uphold the status quo—including the patriarchal domination of men over women. And this is what sexual harassment is part of.

But the workings of the capitalist system stir up forces and contradictions that tend to undermine its stability. Over the last several decades millions of women have been drawn into the workforce, and the sheer number of women working today has drastically changed the workplace and the family in the U.S. Women have also entered many occupations that were male dominated in the past. And at the same time, the ruling classes have unleashed a political and ideological offensive to strengthen the patriarchal relations that are key to social control and the whole private property setup of capitalism.

This has produced a real clash. Working women, especially those in previously male-dominated occupations, have come right up against relations and ways of operating that developed in a situation where women were not around—or were certainly not working as equal co-workers, or even superiors. All the "good ole boy" ways of relating on the job are being threatened by women, and in this situation men have looked for ways to "put women in their place." One way this has expressed itself is through the use of *sex* as a way to exercise power over and threaten women. Through sexual harassment, men devalue a woman's role in the workplace: women are told their worth is to be measured by their appearance, their subservience to others, and in many cases their willingness to submit to sexual advances and even rape. A woman just trying to do her job finds out very quickly that simply because she is a woman and is in the workplace, she is presumed to be "available" and "fair game" for men. She is not evaluated for her skills, creativity, or abilities—but treated like a sexual object. And within the general dog-eat-dog environment of the workplace, sex is used as a powerful way to put women down.

> *"Capitalism is based on private property and the exploitation of labor."*

Sexual harassment is an expression of male domination over women and it is important, for men and women, to understand how this kind of behavior upholds and promotes the oppression of women more generally in society. Even men who are not part of the bourgeois class can act the bourgeoisie by exercising their right to dominate women in this way. Sexual harassment is definitely a *bourgeois* thing, and men who are not about being an oppressor and *are* about fighting for the liberation of women need to thoroughly reject any kind of petty male privileges which allow them to act the bourgeois patriarch—whether it's in the home or on the job.

Built into the System

Some people have said that with all the public debate around sexual harassment, things will get better in the workplace—that companies and men at work (even senators!) will now be more "sensitive" to this problem. But the fact is, there is no way this system can really deal with the problem of sexual harassment.

First of all, it is not in the interest of this system to combat sexual harassment.

The whole ideology behind this kind of behavior is a built-in part of how this system functions and operates. Male domination is part of the foundation of the economic and social relations in this capitalist society. So even though sexual harassment is now against the law and workplaces are required to have policies prohibiting sexual harassment—this system can't solve this problem. The *best* this system can offer is a completely ineffective law and a hypocritical double standard: On one hand sexual harassment is illegal and those

> *"It is very hard, if not impossible, for women to get any kind of justice."*

who get caught *may* be punished. But on the other hand, the entire society is producing and promoting the values and relations that give rise to this behavior.

There have been a few well-publicized cases of women winning big settlements in sexual harassment suits. But these cases are not how things go down for millions of women who face sexual harassment.

Even in instances where lawsuits are filed, women speak of profound embarrassment, reprisals and fear that their career and reputation will suffer, even if they win. And in the majority of cases, filing an official claim proves to be a dead end. For instance, look at how the EEOC (Equal Employment Opportunity Commission) has dealt with sexual harassment claims. This is the official government agency (the one Clarence Thomas headed) that is supposed to enforce federal laws against sexual harassment. Under Title VII of the Civil Rights Act of 1964, anyone who wishes to pursue a charge of sexual harassment, or any other form of employment discrimination, must file a charge with the EEOC. The agency then investigates and decides whether it will sue on behalf of the individual. But the EEOC actually filed suits in only 50 of the 5,694 sexual harassment complaints it received in the fiscal year 1990. In all the other cases, the woman must find a private lawyer (and come up with thousands of dollars to hire this lawyer) to bring the lawsuit to court. And if women file under Title VII they are generally not entitled to damages beyond back pay and reinstatement in their job. Some lawyers who handle sexual harassment cases estimate that, nationwide, no more than 100 cases a year actually get to trial.

Fear of Reporting Harassment

Most of the time women do not even file any kind of claim because they know that if they do they may lose their job or be subject to all kinds of rumors and attacks. Several studies have found that only around *three percent* of women who have been sexually harassed make a formal complaint. And in survey after survey women said they believed that reporting instances of sexual harassment would simply lead to more trouble, that they would not be believed, that they would be labeled as troublemakers or would lose their jobs.

The story of one woman executive in New York is pretty typical. She filed a lawsuit in Federal Court in New York against the subsidiary of one of the country's largest banks, charging in part that it failed to properly address the complaints she filed. The woman said an executive solicited sexual favors, threatening that he would ruin her career if she did not comply. She decided to report the incident "just to get it on the record" but asked the company not to pursue an investigation. Soon after she filed her report, her career degenerated into a succession of demotions, denied transfers, and smaller-than-usual bonuses. Soon after this, the company told her that her job was being terminated.

The fact is, it is very hard, if not impossible, for women to get any kind of justice when they bring to light that they've been sexually harassed on the job. Women are constantly told they should be "team players," that if they want to climb the ladder of success they are going to have to "roll with the punches," sexist jokes and all. In the current climate where reactionary conservatives are attacking affirmative action, there is an ugly wind blowing that claims racist and sexist discrimination doesn't even exist and that women who complain about discrimination and sexual harassment are just trying to get ahead on something other than their qualifications. All this denies that for people of color and women, racism and sexism present real obstacles in the workplace. And all this makes it very hard for women to fight sexual discrimination and harassment on the job.

> *"Only by overthrowing capitalism will it be possible for the masses of people to really deal with sexual harassment."*

Many times sexual harassment goes on "behind closed doors" and women know that if it comes down to their word against a man, especially a supervisor or boss, they won't be believed or will be accused of "fantasizing" or "asking for it." They are threatened and intimidated into not talking by men who have power over salaries, promotions, and firings. And women are put in a position of having to choose between exposing things that are very harmful to them and hurt *all* women or keeping their job. One law professor put it, "Many women tolerate harassment, even though it is debilitating and destructive. The willingness of women to tolerate a hostile work environment often has less to do with how bad the workplace is and more to do with how badly they need their jobs."

This is another example of how capitalist society compels the people to act against the interests of the oppressed in order to survive, and another example of why the oppressed have to rise up and break with the whole bourgeois way of life in order to get liberated.

Struggle Now and in the Future

It will take nothing short of revolution to fundamentally deal with the oppression of women, including sexual harassment on the job. As long as society is based on private property the economic structure in which people work is going to be organized in a way that promotes exploitative and oppressive relationships. And as long as the bourgeoisie rules, an ideology and political program that systematically oppresses women is going to be promoted and enforced throughout society.

Only by overthrowing capitalism will it be possible for the masses of people to really deal with sexual harassment and root out the ideology behind this behavior. Only then will it be possible for there to be the kind of mass debate, discussion and struggle around these questions that will actually lead to transforming the situation—led by the proletariat which is the only class that has no interest in maintaining any form of oppression. In this situation all the institutions in society—the schools, cultural forums, the workplace, etc.—will be organized in a whole new way that promotes real relations of equality. And throughout society there will be struggle to remold people's thinking on these questions and struggle with men to do self-criticism and change their male-chauvinist ideas and behavior.

Women's Rage

The furor around sexual harassment has revealed a pervasive, deep and ugly part of this society. It is a good thing that there is widespread debate and struggle over this issue and revolutionaries have a responsibility to enter into this debate and shed some revolutionary light on this whole subject. In all the different battles today against the oppression of women, there are real opportunities to bring forward the rage of millions of women who hate this system. And this is a tremendous strength in the struggle for women's liberation and for the revolution as a whole.

The Sexual Revolution Caused Sexual Harassment

by George A. Kendall

About the author: *George A. Kendall is a free-lance writer and contributor to* the Wanderer, *a weekly Catholic newspaper.*

We have had incredible quantities of nonsense (to use the polite term) regarding "sexual harassment" dumped on us since the unspeakable Ms. Hill's accusations on that score against Supreme Court nominee Clarence Thomas. As always happens when we allow the far left, and in particular the feminists, to define an issue, little or no rational debate has taken place because the nature of the issue has been distorted beyond all recognition in the public consciousness.

The problem underlying the issue of "sexual harassment," according to various and assorted feminist harpies, is the male use of sexuality, especially in the workplace, to assert and maintain power over women. This amounts to saying that this issue, in accordance with the Marxist paradigm which still dominates the thinking of the left today (despite its rejection by the people who have actually had to live with it) is reducible to the warfare between oppressors and oppressed, with men filling the first role, women the second.

Rational Debate Is Impossible

I would submit that this understanding badly distorts the issue and makes rational debate impossible, substituting for it the cacophony of shrill accusations by alleged victims and angry denials by alleged oppressors which dominated the Thomas hearings. That does not mean "sexual harassment" is an entirely fictitious issue. Underlying the urge to talk about things like "sexual harassment" is an awareness, however confused, that something really is terribly wrong with us in the area of sexuality, that people, in their lives as sexual beings, as men and women, are doing terrible harm to one another. What is really at issue is the prevalence of exploitive sexual relationships in our present-day

George A. Kendall, "Sexual Harassment: How Not to Define an Issue," *The Wanderer*, January 9, 1992. Reprinted with permission.

society, a society formed by the "sexual revolution" of the 1960s.

A few days after the Thomas hearings CNN gave a program on "sexual harassment." This program featured a brief skit purporting to depict a situation which could be construed as sexual harassment in the workplace. An attractive young secretary is warned by her boss against dating co-workers, though there is no actual company policy against doing so.

> *"People, in their lives as sexual beings, as men and women, are doing terrible harm to one another."*

She ignores his advice and, being a liberated woman, asks out a young man in another department. They have a relationship which lasts about six months and presumably includes sex. He visits her in her office during all his coffee breaks and lunch hours. At the end of this time, she decides she is bored with him and drops him. He is frantically in love with her and will not accept that decision. So he continues to contact her every day trying to persuade her to continue the relationship. He continues to come to her work area every lunch hour and coffee break in the effort to win her back. He wants her to marry him. She says that he is crazy, that she has never had the slightest interest in marrying him, and, in effect, doesn't feel it is her fault that he got such a crazy idea.

The secretary believes that she is the victim of sexual harassment and wants her boss to do something to make him cease and desist. The boss understandably feels that the situation is not his concern. After all, he advised her against dating co-workers, and thinks that if she chose to ignore his advice she has to take the consequences. It is *her* problem.

Among other things, this case illustrates what a tremendous oversimplification the feminist propaganda—which sees situations like this solely in terms of victims and victimizers, with men always the victimizers and women always the victims—truly is. The most obvious question that occurs to any intelligent person after considering the case is: Who is really the victim here, anyway? We have here a case in which a woman initiates a relationship, in effect seduces a man, allows him to fall in love with her (something that was quite predictable), then unceremoniously dumps him, leaving him to struggle with the emotional chaos created by her actions. It is perfectly understandable that he is distraught as a result of her decision, and does not want to let go.

Woman as Victimizer

Feminists will never acknowledge this, of course, because despite their theoretical insistence on equality of the sexes, they consistently apply double standards to matters such as this. If a man seduces a woman, gets her to sleep with him, then, after she has fallen in love with him, tells her he is bored with her and dumps her, nearly everyone, feminists included, will agree that he is a louse (using, again, the polite term). Yet when the same situation occurs, with the woman as the victimizer, they will deny the man's right even to feel hurt, let alone give any expression to his anger.

Of course, the young man's actions, while understandable, are immature. If I had to advise him, I would tell him to try to forget the girl, who obviously isn't much of a human being, anyway, and would make a terrible wife, and look for someone better. Needless to say, I would also advise him that the emotional suffering he is undergoing as a result of this vicious relationship is a strong indicator of the soundness of the Christian teaching against extramarital sex, and urge him to adopt Christian moral principles. If I were his boss, I would tell him to stop pestering the girl, not because his acts amount to sexual harassment, but because they are (presumably) disruptive to the functioning of the office.

The young man's instinctive, gut-level reaction to the situation is, nevertheless, a perfectly sound one. Without, in all probability, explicitly articulating it, he knows, somehow, that when two people, married or not, get sexually involved with each other, they create a relationship, one in which they assume responsibility for and toward one another, and thus they acquire obligations toward one another. That, the reader may remember, is one reason why St. Paul condemned fornication—because, even outside marriage, when a man and woman engage in sexual intercourse, they become one flesh, and a sensible person ought to be very careful with whom he or she becomes one flesh. Becoming one flesh with a prostitute, or with another man's wife, or with someone who is likely to exploit you for sexual pleasure and then drop you, can be disastrous, morally, physically, and spiritually.

The Madness of the Sexual Revolution

The real issue is not sexual harassment as the feminists understand it. It is the "sexual revolution." We are encountering the kinds of problems that our opinion-makers describe as "sexual harassment" because the ideological madness about sex implicit in the sexual revolution is beginning to bear fruit, producing disastrous consequences. We are finding, not at all surprisingly, from the Church's standpoint, that unlimited sexual freedom without responsibility causes a great deal of pain and suffering. The idea that anyone, male or female, has the right to whimsically confer sexual favors on another, then withdraw them, equally whimsically, cannot help but create enormous human misery.

> *"When two people, married or not, get sexually involved with each other, they . . . acquire obligations toward one another."*

In the abstract, the idea may sound very plausible that human beings, rather than be tied down to an oppressive, patriarchal institution like marriage, which

79

requires permanent, exclusive commitments, can instead be happy simply moving from casual "relationship" to casual "relationship." This overlooks the reality that these relationships must end some way or other, and usually at least one person is hurt, sometimes grievously.

It is very easy for these situations to lead even to murder or suicide. The newspapers treat us to daily incidents of one or the other. Even the person who casually ends the relationship, without regard for the other person's feelings, is hurt, if only because that person is further dehumanized, further tarnished spiritually by the movement away from love, which is man's participation in the life of God, toward imprisonment within himself. Human nature instinctively rebels against this kind of insanity. When our society rejects this instinctive reaction and further institutionalizes such relationships, then we produce a pervasive atmosphere of sexual exploitation and sadistic callousness toward the persons exploited.

> *"We need to . . . devote some time to serious reflection on the wisdom of the Judeo-Christian morality."*

It is that atmosphere of exploitation, which devalues the human person by making him or her merely an object to be used for one's own pleasure, that we ought to be fighting against, not a poorly defined, fuzzy notion of "sexual harassment." Those cases of "sexual harassment" which ought really to be condemned, such as the boss who makes clear to a female employee that she had better sleep with him if she wants to keep her job or get promoted, are merely one example of the kind of behavior that inevitably gets to be more and more common in a society which refuses to order human sexuality in accord with God's commandment of love.

Since the feminists themselves have rejected Christian moral teaching and wholeheartedly welcomed the sexual revolution, making it a cornerstone of their movement, it is difficult to see how they can possibly object to such harassment. It is their own offspring, whether legitimate or illegitimate.

In the wake of the Thomas hearings, bureaucrats and politicians everywhere are competing to see who can first come up with the largest collection of laws and federal regulations regulating the minutiae of male-female behavior. That route can only lead to totalitarianism. We need to forget all that, and instead devote some time to serious reflection on the wisdom of the Judeo-Christian morality which, by insisting that sex be used only in the context of lifelong marital relationships grounded in a love which mirrors that of the Holy Trinity itself, did so much to spare us the appalling evils that inevitably occur when we reduce sex to the egocentric pursuit of pleasure.

Pornography Encourages Sexual Harassment

by Robert L. Allen

About the author: *Robert L. Allen is a writer in Oakland, California and an editor of* The Black Scholar *magazine.*

The furor over charges that Supreme Court then-nominee Clarence Thomas sexually harassed a female assistant, Anita Hill—now a University of Oklahoma law school professor—focused national attention on the issue of sexual harassment. It also compels us to consider pornography.

The dramatic accusation and denial provoked intense debate, but the fact is that thousands of women are sexually harassed every day, a great many of them women of color and poor women who are most vulnerable in the jobs that sexist and racist discrimination forces them to take—farm workers, "domestics," sweatshop and factory workers. Not only are these women especially vulnerable to sexual harassment; they also have less access to the levers of power needed to seek redress. The majority of the crimes against them are not reported because women fear revenge from employers or know their complaint will be dismissed. They are doubly oppressed: subjected to abuse and constrained to remain silent about it.

As an African American man, I am outraged by the sexism and racism that make so many of my sisters who must work to support their families targets for sexual attacks by bosses and supervisors and other men in power.

The Business of Pornography

However, incidents of sexual harassment are not unrelated to the flood of pornography that has invaded even the corner market. Pornography is a multibillion-dollar business. I suspect that for every man who sexually harasses a woman in the workplace there must be hundreds if not thousands of us who occasionally or habitually buy pornography. If questioned, we may rationalize it on the grounds of its being a safe fantasy alternative to unsafe sexual practices (which is exactly what some porn mags now proudly claim to be) and point out that the violence in commercially distributed porn has been eliminated or at least toned down (some mags carry a tag proclaiming their "nonviolent explicit action").

But we cannot continue to evade the recognition that even "tasteful" pornography demeans and degrades women and men by exploiting our sexuality and making a commodity of the most intimate physical connection between two human beings. Studies show that it also elicits sexualized aggression in men who view it, no doubt contributing to the epidemic of sexualized violence against women that stalks our communities. But studies, statistics, and even discussions with friends can be kept at a distance—safely impersonal and intellectual. It becomes possible to separate knowledge from action: an intellectual understanding of pornography as poison having no apparent effect on the practice of using it. But when porn comes home it is harder to evade the contradictions.

> *"Thousands of women are sexually harassed every day, a great many of them women of color and poor women."*

A short time ago I discovered a pornographic magazine tucked under my teenage son's bed. Knowing that pornography is so pervasive, I was not shocked, but finding it was a "soft-core" magazine *I* had purchased bathed me in shame. At first I was tempted to hide my guilty feeling by getting mad at my son and dumping my discomfort on him. Fortunately, a moment's reflection, made possible by the fact that he was not at home when I discovered the magazine, allowed me to think of a better approach. After all, his interest in the magazine stemmed from an adolescent's emerging and normal interest in sex. I decided to tell him I found the magazine and to have a talk with him about sexuality. I also gave him a copy of *The Joy of Sex*. I didn't have the courage to talk about why I had bought the magazine.

Sexual Exploitation

Recently I returned from a trip to New York City. While I was there I took my 18-year-old niece to dinner and we talked about her career. A beautiful and intelligent young woman, she is struggling to succeed in the highly competitive business of professional modeling. It is something she has diligently pursued since as a pre-teen she appeared in amateur fashion shows at the local malls. Of course, the family has been worried about her vulnerability to sexual exploitation by the clients, photographers, and other men with whom she must work. Her mother, who lives in another city, calls every few days to check on her.

My niece showed me her "book," a portfolio showing her in various poses and clothes. Sometimes the clothes were a bit skimpy, but the poses always tasteful. Many of the photos were stunning and vibrant, revealing her youthful beauty and poise. But I became uncomfortable as I thought about how these photos use her body to sell products. Even more discomforting was my realization that for some men the distance between these photos and the images in some of the more "tasteful" porn magazines was not all that great. Knowing of my niece's struggle to make a living, I was sickened by the thought that she might feel pressured to do other kinds of "modeling" to survive. Of course, my niece would never do this, but I was deeply disturbed by the recognition that she might be economically pushed in that direction and that I, as an occasional consumer of pornography, helped create the economic pull that would draw her or others into it.

I hope my niece will be O.K. But the fact is that many young girls are pushed into pornography and prostitution simply to survive. And the racist exploitation of black women and other women of color in pornography and prostitution is notorious. As a black man I feel I must stop being complicit with a system that would demean and degrade my niece and other women I cherish.

Feigned Enjoyment

It is not difficult to truly see (rather than merely ogle) the women (and men) who appear in porn mags. Look at the eyes rather than the body; you will see the pain, the anger, the feigned enjoyment on the women's faces; the vacantness and forced leers on the faces of the men. Even if you look only at the bodies, ask yourself: Are these images the way I want my son to see sexuality, to see women, to see men? Would I want my niece, my daughter, or my partner to be one of the images on the page?

Pornography corrupts our sexuality, our most intimate relations. That is reason enough to consider it a major personal problem. That it also harms women and children and men by fostering aggression and abuse makes it a major social problem. We need to heal the wounds of pornography. Through community education and action, legislative initiative, and support groups for victims of harassment and recovering porn "addicts," the problem must be addressed.

> *"Pornography corrupts our sexuality, our most intimate relations."*

It is time for pornography to come out of its hiding place in the bedroom closet of our collective psyche, and finally—with no second thoughts or lingering doubts—be thrown into the trash.

83

Unclear Laws Make Sexual Harassment More Prevalent

by Naomi Wolf

About the author: *Naomi Wolf is the author of the feminist bestseller* The Beauty Myth.

Recent research consistently shows that inside the majority of the West's controlled, attractive, successful working women, there is a secret "underlife" poisoning our freedom; infused with notions of beauty, it is a dark vein of self-hatred, physical obsessions, terror of aging, and dread of lost control.

It is no accident that so many potentially powerful women feel this way. We are in the midst of a violent backlash against feminism that uses images of female beauty as a political weapon against women's advancement: the beauty myth. It is the modern version of a social reflex that has been in force since the Industrial Revolution. As women released themselves from the feminine mystique of domesticity, the beauty myth took over its lost ground, expanding as it waned to carry on its work of social control.

The contemporary backlash is so violent because the ideology of beauty is the last one remaining of the old feminine ideologies that still has the power to control those women whom second wave feminism would have otherwise made relatively uncontrollable: It has grown stronger to take over the work of social coercion that myths about motherhood, domesticity, chastity, and passivity, no longer can manage. It is seeking right now to undo psychologically and covertly all the good things that feminism did for women materially and overtly.

Countering Feminism

This counterforce is operating to checkmate the inheritance of feminism on every level in the lives of Western women. Feminism gave us laws against job discrimination based on gender; immediately case law evolved in Britain and the United States that institutionalized job discrimination based on women's appearances. . . .

The law developed a tangle of inconsistencies in which women were paralyzed: While one ruling, *Miller* v. *Bank of America*, confused sexual attraction with sexual harassment and held that the law has no part to play in employment disputes that centered on it ("attractiveness," the court decided, being a "natural sex phenomenon" which "plays at least a subtle part in

> *"A judge can look at any younger woman and believe he is seeing a harassable trollop."*

most personnel decisions," and, as such, the court shouldn't delve into "such matters"), the court in another case, *Barnes* v. *Costle*, concluded that if a woman's unique physical characteristics—red hair, say, or large breasts—were the reasons given by her employer for sexual harassment, then her personal appearance was the issue and not her gender, in which case she could not expect protection under Title VII of the 1964 Civil Rights Act. With these rulings a woman's beauty became at once her job and her fault.

United States law developed to protect the interests of the power structure by setting up a legal maze in which the beauty myth blocks each path so that no woman can "look right" and win. [Margarita] St. Cross lost her job because she was too "old" and too "ugly"; [television anchorwoman Christine] Craft lost hers because she was too "old," too "ugly," "unfeminine," and didn't dress right. This means, a woman might think, that the law will treat her fairly in employment disputes if only she does her part, looks pretty, and dresses femininely.

Legal Advice

She would be dangerously wrong, though. Let's look at an American working woman standing in front of her wardrobe, and imagine the disembodied voice of legal counsel advising her on each choice as she takes it out on its hanger.

"Feminine, then," she asks, "in reaction to the Craft decision?"

"You'd be asking for it. In 1986, Mechelle Vinson filed a sex discrimination case in the District of Columbia against her employer, the Meritor Savings Bank, on the grounds that her boss had sexually harassed her, subjecting her to fondling, exposure, and rape. Vinson was young and 'beautiful' and carefully dressed. The district court ruled that her appearance counted against her: Testimony about her 'provocative' dress could be heard to decide whether her harassment was 'welcome.'"

"Did she dress provocatively?"

"As her counsel put it in exasperation, 'Mechelle Vinson wore *clothes.*' Her beauty in her clothes was admitted as evidence to prove that she welcomed rape from her employer."

"Well, feminine, but not too feminine, then."

"Careful: In *Hopkins* v. *Price-Waterhouse*, Ms. Hopkins was denied a partnership because she needed to learn to 'walk more femininely, talk more femininely, dress more femininely,' and 'wear makeup.'"

"Maybe she didn't deserve a partnership?"

"She brought in the most business of any employee."

"Hmm. Well, maybe a little more feminine."

"Not so fast. Policewoman Nancy Fahdl was fired because she looked 'too much like a lady.'"

"All right, less feminine. I've wiped off my blusher."

"You can lose your job if you don't wear makeup. See *Tamini* v. *Howard Johnson Company, Inc.*"

"How about this, then, sort of . . . womanly?"

"Sorry. You can lose your job if you dress like a woman. In *Andre* v. *Bendix Corporation*, it was ruled 'inappropriate for a supervisor' of women to dress like 'a woman.'"

"What am I supposed to do? Wear a sack?"

"Well, the women in *Buren* v. *City of East Chicago* had to 'dress to cover themselves from neck to toe' because the men at work were 'kind of nasty.'"

"Won't a dress code get me out of this?"

"Don't bet on it. In *Diaz* v. *Coleman*, a dress code of short skirts was set by an employer who allegedly sexually harassed his female employees because they complied with it." . . .

Turning the Tables

Beauty provokes harassment, the law says, but it looks through men's eyes when deciding what provokes it. A woman employer may find a well-cut European herringbone twill, wantonly draped over a tautly muscled masculine flank, madly provocative, especially since it suggests male power and status, which our culture eroticizes. But the law is unlikely to see good Savile Row tailoring her way if she tells its possessor he must service her sexually or lose his job.

If, at work, women were under no more pressure to be decorative than are their well-groomed male peers in lawyer's pinstripe or banker's gabardine, the pleasure of the workplace might narrow; but so would a well-tilled field of discrimination. Since women's appearance is used to justify their sexual harassment as well as their dismissal, the statements made by women's clothing are continually, willfully misread. Since women's working clothes—high heels, stockings, makeup, jewelry, not to mention hair, breasts, legs, and hips—have already been appropriated as pornographic accessories, a judge can look at any younger woman and

"A woman's beauty became at once her job and her fault."

believe he is seeing a harassable trollop, just as he can look at any older woman and believe he is seeing a dismissable hag.

Emulating the male uniform *is* tough on women. Their urge to make traditionally masculine space less gray, sexless, and witless is an appealing wish. But their contribution did not relax the rules. Men failed to respond with whimsy, costume, or color of their own. The consequence of men wearing uniforms where women do not has simply meant that women take on the *full* penalties as well as the pleasures of physical charm in the workplace, and can legally be punished or promoted, insulted or even raped accordingly.

> *"The beauty myth blocks each path so that no woman can 'look right' and win."*

Women dare not yet relinquish the "advantage" this inequality in dress bestows. People put on uniforms voluntarily only when they have faith in the fair rewards of the system. They will understandably be unwilling to give up the protection of their "beauty" until they can be sure the reward system is in good working order; the professions will be unwilling to give up the controlling function of the professional beauty qualification until they are certain that women are so demoralized by it that they will pose no real threat to the way things are done. It's an uneasy truce, each side playing for time; however, when playing for time under the beauty myth, women lose.

What about the common perception that women use their "beauty" to get ahead? In fact, sociologist Barbara A. Gutek shows that there is little evidence that women even occasionally use their sexuality to get some organizational reward. It is men, she found, who use their sexuality to get ahead: "A sizeable minority of men," she found, "say they dress in a seductive manner at work," versus 1 woman in 800 who said she had used sexuality for advancement. In another study, 35 percent of men versus only 15 percent of women say that they use their appearance for rewards in the workplace.

Feminine Wiles

Complicity in display does exist, of course. Does that mean the women are to blame for it? I have heard Ivy League administrators, judges discussing women attorneys, scholarship panelists, and other men employed to believe in and enforce concepts of fairness speak complacently about the uses of "feminine wiles"—a euphemism for beauty deployed to the woman's advantage. Powerful men characterize them with grudging admiration, as if "beauty's" power were an irresistible force that stunned and immobilized distinguished men, to turn them into putty in the charmer's hand. This attitude makes sure that women will have to keep using the things they sometimes use to try to get the things they seldom get.

The conventions of this gallantry are veils over the inscription in stone: It is the powerful who dictate the terms; adults, playwrestling a child, enjoy letting the child feel it has won.

This point, where beauty forms the bridge between women and institutions, is what women are taught to seize upon, and is then used as proof that women themselves are finally to blame. But to make herself grasp at this straw, a woman has to suppress what she knows: that the powerful ask for women to display themselves in this way. When power toys with beauty, the request for display behavior has been choreographed before the woman has had the chance to enter the room where she will be evaluated.

No Choice

This request for display behavior is unspoken. It is subtle enough so that the woman cannot point to it, credibly, as an example of harassment (to be credible about being harassed, in any case, a woman must look harassable, which destroys her credibility). It usually leaves the toyed-with "beauty" no choice, short of a withdrawal so obvious as to give certain offense, but to play along. She may have to will her body to relax and not stiffen at an untoward compliment, or simply have to sit up straighter, letting her body be seen more clearly, or brush the hair from her eyes in a way that she knows flatters her face. Whatever it is she has to do, she knows it without being told, from the expression and body language of the powerful man in whose eyes her future lies.

> *"The powerful ask for women to display themselves in this way."*

When a brilliant critic and a beautiful woman (that's my order of priorities, not necessarily those of the men who teach her) puts on black suede spike heels and a ruby mouth before asking an influential professor to be her thesis advisor, is she a slut? Or is she doing her duty to herself, in a clear-eyed appraisal of a hostile or indifferent milieu, by taking care to nourish her real gift under the protection of her incidental one? Does her hand shape the lipstick into a cupid's bow in a gesture of free will?

She doesn't have to do it.

That is the response the beauty myth would like a woman to have, because then the Other Woman is the enemy. Does she in fact have to do it?

Future Alternatives

The aspiring woman does not have to do it if she has a choice. She will have a choice when a plethora of faculties in her field, headed by women and endowed by generations of female magnates and robber baronesses, open their gates to her; when multinational corporations led by women clamor for the skills of young female graduates; when there are *other* universities, with bronze busts of the heroines of half a millennium's classical learning; when there are *other* research-funding boards maintained by the deep coffers provided by the revenues of female inventors, where half the chairs are held by women scientists. She'll have a choice when her application is evaluated blind.

Women will have the choice never to stoop, and will deserve the full censure for stooping, to consider what the demands on their "beauty" of a board of power might be, the minute they know they can count on their fair share: that 52 percent of the seats of the highest achievement are open to them. They will deserve the blame that they now get anyway only when they know that the best dream of their one life will not be forcibly compressed into an inverted pyramid, slammed up against a glass ceiling, shunted off into a stifling pink-collar ghetto, shoved back dead down a dead-end street.

Chapter 3

How Can Sexual Harassment Be Reduced?

Chapter Preface

Even before Anita Hill took the stand during the hearings for Supreme Court nominee Clarence Thomas, sexual harassment had become a topic of concern in large organizations like businesses, hospitals, schools, and the military. These organizations have seen an increase in sexual harassment cases and are now spending time and money searching for ways to reduce the problem.

Many experts on sexual harassment advocate three important steps in reducing sexual harassment in any institution. One is to create an atmosphere that explicitly rejects sexual harassment as acceptable behavior. Another is to provide a means of communication for victims of sexual harassment to come forward with their complaints. The last is to establish an efficient policy for investigating and resolving the complaints.

While few argue that these methods would not help reduce sexual harassment, some experts query the necessity for any anti-harassment policies. These critics contend that sexual harassment and other kinds of inappropriate behavior are unfortunate but common occurrences in the work world. Gretchen Morgenson, a senior editor for *Forbes*, states, "No woman should have to run a daily gauntlet of sexual innuendo, but neither is it reasonable for women to expect a pristine work environment free of coarse behavior." Experts such as Morgenson argue that, in most cases, confronting the harasser and telling him or her to stop is the most effective way to reduce harassment.

The viewpoints in the following chapter discuss ways to reduce sexual harassment.

Strict Anti-Harassment Policies Can Reduce Sexual Harassment in Business

by Alan Deutschman

About the author: *Alan Deutschman is an associate editor for* Fortune, *a bi-weekly business magazine.*

Who could watch the controversy surrounding Clarence Thomas and Anita Hill without wondering how a case alleging sexual harassment might be handled in his or her own office? How to respond if you are preyed upon, or if you, as a manager, are charged to investigate an allegation? Says Labor Secretary Lynn Martin: "If any good comes from the Thomas situation, it will only be a wider discussion of the issue of harassment." That issue, always sensitive, has become increasingly subtle and confusing as legal definitions of harassment expand from obvious barbarities to encompass acts that over time create a "hostile work environment."

Corporations Are Getting Tough

Business stands on the front line in the battle against harassment, pushed there by judicial decisions in the 1980s that hold employers financially liable for workers' transgressions unless the company actively strives to prevent offenses and responds effectively when they occur. As a result, corporations are getting tough about the subject: crafting intensive seminars for employees, such as those that take place at Honeywell and Corning; establishing 24-hour hotlines and providing security for victims fearful of reprisals, as Du Pont does; and initiating and completing inquiries swiftly, as AT&T strives to do.

The results? No big gains so far—it may be early, and there are precious few data from the past to compare with. But the experience of large organizations at work on change offers valuable lessons for any company or concerned employee.

While even a single case of harassment is one too many, the extent of the problem may be overblown, particularly in assertions that 75% or 90% of women have been victimized. The most authoritative data on the pervasiveness of harassment in its various guises come from the U.S. Merit Systems Protection Board, a federal agency. In 1980 it polled 20,000 federal employees about the incidence of sexual harassment in government offices. It repeated the survey in 1987, asking the same questions of another 8,500 government workers. The results of both polls were remarkably similar: 1% of female respondents claimed to be victims of actual or attempted rape or assault: 6% reported pressure for sexual favors.

"Educating employees is vital but not easy, because there is considerable uncertainty and disagreement about what harassment is."

Only a few incidents involved a boss demanding a quid pro quo from a subordinate—have sex with me if you want that promotion or want to keep your job. Most incidents occurred between peers or colleagues. In these cases job security isn't at stake, but the work environment can become abusive. Offensive conduct, according to the women polled, took the form of remarks (cited by 35% of women), suggestive looks (28%), touching (26%), pressure for dates (15%), and unwanted love letters and calls (12%). Men suffered all the same kinds of harassment, but the incidence was about a third that of women. Men were far less apt to talk about it or report it to supervisors.

Likely Victims

Merit Systems found that the most likely victims—female or male—were single or divorced. Women were at above-average risk if they had college educations or graduate degrees; men, if they worked in clerical jobs. The risk was also higher for workers in places where the vast majority of their coworkers were of the opposite sex.

Harassment isn't just a matter of one employee's victimizing another. Clients and customers can also use the power of their position—go along or I'll give the sale to somebody else—as a license for licentiousness, especially in such fields as law, consulting, and advertising. In a 1989 *National Law Journal* survey of 900 female attorneys, 10% said that clients exerted unwanted pressure for dates, 9% complained of touching, cornering, or pinching, and 4% cited pressure for sex, sometimes as a prerequisite for getting the client's business.

So what should a company do to keep its employees—and itself—safe? Educating employees is vital but not easy, because there is considerable uncertainty and disagreement about what harassment is. Legal doctrine has evolved fitfully since the landmark 1986 Supreme Court decision *Meritor Savings Bank v. Vinson*. That case expanded the definition of harassment to include verbal or physical conduct that creates an intimidating, hostile, or offensive work environment or unreasonably interferes with an employee's job performance.

Unfortunately, men and women harbor different notions of what's intimidating, hostile, or offensive. A survey conducted in 1981 by sociologist Barbara Gutek of 1,200 people in Los Angeles County found that 67% of the men said they would feel flattered if a colleague of the opposite sex propositioned them, while 63% of women would be offended. Another survey by *Redbook* magazine and *Harvard Business Review* indicated that 24% of the women believed that a man giving a female worker a visual once-over was harassment, while only 8% of men thought so.

The best corporate practice calls for companies to create and publicize a forceful policy against sexual harassment. In 1989, Honeywell clarified its once obscure and legalistic harassment statement by distributing handbooks in plain English to every employee and putting up posters in conspicuous places. As a result the number of reported incidents has increased significantly, a good sign suggesting that more victims are seeking help.

Corporate education programs typically start out by sensitizing employees to the issue of harassment and then use role playing or other techniques to rehearse tactics to counter it. Du Pont's efforts are a worthy model. In 1988 the company began

> *"Men and women harbor different notions of what's intimidating, hostile, or offensive."*

offering its employees a four-hour workshop on harassment called "A Matter of Respect." So far 65,000 workers have gone through it. Explains Dar Di Sabatino, a director of the workshop: "We were hearing about subtle situations of harassment. The individuals didn't know what they could do about it or if they should do anything about it." Each workshop is led by a specially trained man and woman; these teams are recruited from all areas of the company, not just from human relations. Small groups—always a balanced mix of men and women—watch videos portraying incidents that can be from real life, then discuss appropriate responses.

The Direct Approach Is Best

The simplest and most effective way to put an end to harassment in most instances is to ask or tell the person to stop. This just-say-knock-it-off tactic worked for 61% of the women who tried it, according to the Merit Systems survey. Telling other colleagues, or simply threatening to do so, proved the second-best response, effective 55% of the time. Pretending to ignore the offensive behavior—a common ploy—usually doesn't work at all.

When employees can't resolve the situation on their own, or feel unsure about what to do, employers should make it easy and safe for them to seek help. Since 1985, Du Pont has run a unique 24-hour hotline that offers advice on personal security and sexual harassment. Callers need not identity themselves, calling does not constitute bringing charges, and confidentiality is assured. "The hotline is a real source of comfort," says Di Sabatino. "It gives people direction and helps them think the issues through before they take any action."

Quick Action

If a victim of or witness to harassment lodges an official complaint, there must be an immediate response. At Du Pont, the employee's supervisor usually handles the matter, but if he or she is the accused, or the employee feels uncomfortable talking to the supervisor, a personnel specialist can do the job. Sometimes a full-fledged investigation may be necessary. Alas, fact finding is often difficult or impossible, since there may not be any witnesses or physical evidence of harassment. Paula Winkler, who looks into charges for AT&T, which, like Du Pont, has a policy of immediate investigation, observes that another problem is proving the sexual attention was unwanted. "One of the first questions we ask the victim," she says, "is, 'Did you tell the person you didn't like it, and how many times?' "

Quick action is essential. In the early 1980s the federal government took an average of 482 days to resolve a harassment complaint filed by one of its employees. Not surprisingly, many victims said they lacked confidence in the system and didn't enlist its aid. Winkler says AT&T strives to complete its inquiries in three to 20 days. Even that period can seem nerve-rackingly long: Du Pont sometimes engages security guards to prevent retaliation against complainants during investigations.

If allegations are proved, companies must find an appropriate response—from warnings to reassignment to termination of the offender. Du Pont automatically reassigns the harasser unless the victim specifically requests a transfer.

Occasionally the accuser is the guilty party. Winkler estimates that some 5% of allegations at AT&T prove false. They are commonly the work of employees taking revenge against a boss—often following a disappointing performance review— or conniving to switch departments.

> *"Sexual harassment tends to be less common in stable companies where employees feel some loyalty to the corporation."*

AT&T suggests that these people go through counseling, and some companies subject them to penalties, such as demotion.

A final, and timely, word of warning: Sexual harassment tends to be less common in stable companies where employees feel some loyalty to the corporation and to one another. They realize they must treat everyone with respect and sensitivity, if only because they are all going to be working together a long time. One ugly consequence of restructuring and recession is that they may jeopardize that kind of stability, creating work environments more conducive to harassment.

Men Must Reexamine Their Attitudes to Reduce Sexual Harassment

by Ruth Rosen

About the author: *Ruth Rosen is a history professor at the University of California, Davis, a columnist for the* Los Angeles Times, *and the author of the book* The Lost Sisterhood: Prostitution in America.

One of the many questions people still ask, months after the Clarence Thomas hearings, is: Why didn't Anita Hill come forward earlier? Many harassed women still haven't. Let's remember our history. Until the late 1970s, when feminist legal theorists coined the term sexual harassment, women possessed no language with which to describe these offenses. We just felt offended or violated. We kept silent because we wanted to keep our jobs, we dreaded publicity, and we feared our integrity would be impugned. True, by the time Anita Hill worked for Clarence Thomas, the idea of sexual harassment had entered legal discourse. But it was not yet illegal.

Whether or not Anita Hill's allegations are true, there are good reasons why they are persuasive. About half of all working women have experienced some form of sexual harassment. Judge Thomas, moreover, forfeited his credibility when he repudiated long-held conservative principles in order to win confirmation votes.

The Author's Experience

Some men think sexual harassment is an insignificant breach; I'd like to counter with a true story. At a film screening, I spotted a white-haired professor emeritus in the audience. For twenty-two years, I had never confronted him. As soon as he recognized me, he greeted me with flattering remarks about my ca-

Ruth Rosen, "Sex, Lies, and Vulnerability," *Tikkun*, January/February 1992. Reprinted with permission of *Tikkun: A Bimonthly Jewish Critique of Politics, Culture, and Society*, 5100 Leona St., Oakland, CA 94619, 1-800-877-5231; subscriptions $31/year.

reer. Suddenly, I heard myself say: "I will never forgive you for trying to destroy my career." He looked genuinely shocked. A veteran womanizer, he could not recall what I could not forget.

In 1969, I was a young graduate student in a program I intended to transfer out of after I received my master's degree. The department nevertheless admitted me to the doctoral program. Soon afterward, this professor, the chair of my thesis committee, repeatedly called and asked me out on dates. I refused consistently.

> *"Millions of working women experienced sexual harassment long before we knew what to call it."*

Several weeks later, I received notice that I had not been advanced to the doctoral program after all, and I wondered what had happened. A secretary in the department confided to me that this professor had suddenly protested my acceptance to the program. When I asked him why, he coolly told me I wasn't "Ph.D. material."

If I had wanted to pursue this field, my career would have ended right then. My confidence was severely undermined. Fortunately, the history department, where I wished to transfer, immediately accepted my application for the doctoral program.

Around 1982, when Clarence Thomas became chair of the Equal Employment Opportunity Commission, I finally realized I had been a victim of sexual harassment. This man had intentionally punished me for refusing his advances. A big supporter of liberal causes, he often showed up at faculty benefits or meetings I attended. My body always stiffened with rage, but still I said nothing. Even today, I won't reveal his name. This is not because I want to protect him, but because he is retired, cannot harm other students, and does not seek a lifetime appointment on the Supreme Court. Like Anita Hill, I prefer my privacy to scandal. I also want to make a larger point: Millions of working women experienced sexual harassment long before we knew what to call it.

Anita Hill's Credibility

What still shocks me is that *the* moment of truth during the hearings was so widely ignored. Because Anita Hill testified during the day, rather than during prime time, one of the most important facts was lost amid more lurid details. Anita Hill was asked if the FBI report of her last dinner with Clarence Thomas was accurate. The report was damning: It said that Thomas threatened to ruin *her* career if she made a case against him for what had happened at the EEOC. In careful, precise language, Anita Hill refuted the FBI report. That's not what he said, she testified. He said that if she told anyone, it would hurt *his* career.

At that moment, Anita Hill's credibility should have been secured forever. She could have agreed with the FBI report. It accused Thomas of the most egregious kind of coercion—threatening to destroy an employee's career—which would have amounted to a charge of blackmail, a felony. But Anita Hill didn't let that charge stand. She corrected the record and diminished the crime—for which she could have had no other motive than to tell the truth.

No Democrat picked up on Hill's refutation. Amid all the charges and countercharges, Hill's commitment to accuracy, her unwillingness to charge Thomas falsely, was ignored. Even her defenders on the Senate Judiciary Committee ignored this decisive moment. Most people have never heard or read about the most convincing reasons why they should have believed Anita Hill's testimony.

Men now feel a new kind of vulnerability in offices around the country. Many men are confused about what constitutes sexual harassment. How should I behave? they ask. I don't like this infringement on my speech and action, they gripe. It's a woman's problem, not mine.

In many ways, these complaints signal that the hearings actually rattled many men's consciousness. Men *should* be confused, because too many male co-workers have never before considered a woman's point of view. If men must now suffer a temporary period of self-consciousness, it will perhaps afford them a glimpse into the reality of women's daily lives. We are supposed to look attractive, yet we must also plan how to dress to avoid the possibility of street rape or harassment. We worry about how we should act in order to prevent date rape. We tip-toe around husbands' egos to avoid domestic violence. Much of the female experience is riddled with painful self-consciousness.

Men Need to Think

Men might rethink their behavior by consulting their female co-workers. When a male colleague turns up in the office looking particularly sharp, we say, "You look great today." We know how to compliment an individual without embarrassing anyone and without issuing a sexual invitation.

If men are still confused, I suggest the following thought experiment: Imagine your daughter, sister, or mother at work. How do you want her male co-workers to address her, to compliment her, to treat her? What kind of behavior would enrage you? What words would make your blood boil? Reflect on your answers and you'll know how to treat your female co-workers.

> *"Men now feel a new kind of vulnerability in offices around the country."*

Feminists, for their part, have rarely recognized that rage is the least effective way to convince men of women's needs. Recrimination against men in the abstract will not create peaceful coexistence at the workplace. Sometimes, the quickest way to a man's heart is not through his stomach, as we were taught, but through his concern for the women he loves.

During and after the hearings, thousands of women swapped stories of past sexual harassment. At the State University of New York, Buffalo, women faculty and students organized a speak-out at which women spilled tales they had buried for twenty or thirty years. On countless op-ed pages, women described—often for the first time—the sexual blackmail they had experienced and explained why they, too, had never told a soul.

Anita Hill ignited a national discussion that was long overdue. We have realized that we must redraw the boundaries of what constitutes acceptable behavior; so far, no national consensus has emerged. Sex is not the same as sexism; sexual attention is not the same thing as sexual harassment. It is not harassment to tell a woman she looks nice or ask her out for a date. It *is* harassment to leer, snicker, insult, not take no for an answer, make a woman's work environment inhospitable, or threaten her job. In the end, I think we will all agree that sexual harassment can be avoided if we remember the purpose of etiquette: to avoid offending another individual's feelings.

While we thrash through these questions of gender protocol, this much remains clear: Whatever the political and cultural fallout from the hearings, sexual harassment has ceased to be just a "women's issue" and has entered mainstream national politics. In the years to come, many men will learn what women already know: that sexual harassment is not a compliment. It is a violation of the law.

A Revival of Feminism Can Reduce Sexual Harassment

by Naomi Wolf

About the author: *Naomi Wolf, a feminist activist, is the author of* The Beauty Myth.

This is not a piece about sexual harassment, because the Hill-Thomas confrontation is no more about sexual harassment alone than the storming of the Bastille was simply a breach of prison security.

Women will remember where they were when Anita Hill began speaking. This is not only a case about two individuals and what may, or may not, have happened between them, as serious as those allegations are. Lawmakers are stumbling about in unfamiliar territory, and many women are watching with a sense of unfolding history, because the ideology of gender in America may be at stake.

Hill's charges, and the Senate's response, exposed the status of American women on three levels. We all understand the first: A great many women have been sexually harassed on the job. Four out of 10 women reported experiences of sexual harassment in a *New York Times*/CBS News poll; a 1981 survey of women federal employees found that 43 percent had experienced harassment; and Catharine MacKinnon's groundbreaking study, "Sexual Harassment of Working Women," reports that two-thirds of working women had been sexually harassed. The hearings, as Republican Sen. Arlen Specter of Pennsylvania observed, "have raised the consciousness of America" with regard to this situation.

The System Has Failed Women

The remaining revelations offered by the Hill-Thomas case transcend sexual transgressions: They expose the failure of our political system to work on behalf of women, and they highlight the way in which economic pressure from the male-dominated workplace has helped to paralyze feminism as a broad-

Naomi Wolf, "Stirring the Women's Movement from Its Dormant Decade," *The Washington Post National Weekly Edition*, October 21-27, 1991. Reprinted with permission.

101

based social movement over the past decade.

The insights that we can glean already from the case could turn women, who as a pressure group have been less effective than the National Rifle Association, into a lobby as potent as its potential membership: half the land.

As for our unresponsive politics, the Judiciary Committee's initial failure to act decisively on the FBI report revealed to women what senators have had to struggle suddenly to understand: that women are routinely betrayed by systems of redress for injury and representation of interests made dysfunctional by gender bias. Women's outrage at their cavalier treatment as voters transcends party politics: Republican women in the work force are just as likely to be harassed as are Democratic women.

> *"It's hard to pull yourself up by the bootstraps when your boss has his hand up your leg."*

Both are enraged . . . at the way in which the issue was initially handled. Sexual harassment goes to the root of conservative women's own ideology: It's hard to pull yourself up by the bootstraps when your boss has his hand up your leg.

And liberal women are incensed by the irony of the setting—the Equal Employment Opportunity Commission, where Thomas and Hill were colleagues—of some of the alleged harassment, including not only the incident that Hill alleges but other cases brought up during the hearings. If Hill's charges have merit, they will confirm, in Hogarthian detail, what many women suspect: that the machinery of checks and balances meant to protect their equality is not in working order. In the Reagan years, the arena established to safeguard women's equality became a stage set.

Betraying Women

The Senate's initial bungling amounts to a civic betrayal of women. What is most charitably described as the committee's blunder demonstrates to women that a legislative body composed of only men is virtually as useless to them as would be a straightforward policy of gender apartheid.

When 98 out of 100 senators are male, you have a governing body that, in this case, failed to credibly represent the concerns of the majority of Americans who are female—or even, it appears, pick these concerns out of a lineup.

This case is of revolutionary significance not only for women; it has already proven to be a turning point for men on Capitol Hill. Whatever its outcome, they have been forced to deal with the political reality of women's outrage, as it has expressed itself in a deluge of telephone calls to Capitol Hill offices, sinking approval ratings for Judge Thomas and protests by women who hold elective office on the Hill too. Until now, the harassment of women in the face of a united male front has always been systematized; the old boy network has never before malfunctioned so embarrassingly.

This case could prove to be the sexists' Waterloo. After all, it is a nightmare of chauvinist anxiety: What if you had an alleged victim who won't be silent— who has firmness, conviction and a Yale law degree? What if the no-longer all-male press refuses to be satisfied with the usual stonewalling? If your constituents suddenly identify along gender rather than along party lines, what script do you follow?

Sexual harassment is, according to one top female official, "the culture of the Hill." "Half the guys up there lamenting now what a serious charge this is had their hands on some underpaid female aide last week," she says. What if that army of beleaguered aides were to speak up? . . .

The Hill-Thomas case provides an important insight into the fate of American feminism; specifically why, after flourishing in the activist 1970s, it was driven underground to stagnate, at least in the mainstream, throughout the individualist 1980s.

If Anita Hill told the Judiciary Committee the truth, then she has kept silent for 10 years. This apparent decade-long silence of hers, and the quarter-century silence of Frances Conley, the Stanford neurosurgeon whose sexual harassment became public when she abruptly resigned her several posts, are representative of the general silencing of women's issues in the male-dominated workplace.

Why Women Remain Silent

Hill, when asked what kept her quiet, responded, "I wanted to stay in civil rights. I thought I had something to add." Conley replied to the same question, "I thought I'd be a good neurosurgeon." Georgetown law professor Emma Coleman Jordan summed it up in an article in the *New York Times*. "Keep silent," she wrote, "or risk destroying the hard-won gains of years of education and rigorous training."

No woman should be judged for whatever decision leads her to keep silent. I've been hearing variations of such silence across America. It extends far beyond the tolerance of specific episodes of sexual harassment, and into many women's public disavowal of attitudes that could be construed by their employers as feminist. While traveling from state to state, to listen to audiences of ambitious, educated middle-class women explore why they often don't identify with the women's movement, I have begun to ask them about professional punishment for holding feminist beliefs.

"A legislative body composed of only men is virtually as useless to them as would be a straightforward policy of gender apartheid."

It is at this point that heads begin to nod in affirmation. If I am interviewing women in an office building, it is also at this point that I'm drawn behind closed doors. They tell their stories and ask not to be identified.

"I know my limits," says a television producer. "I know what they will let me get away with," says a graduate student. "You walk a fine line," says a magazine editor. "If I make any kind of feminist fuss, there are 50 of me waiting in the wings to take my place," says a radio programmer. One young woman, who is putting up with sexual harassment to keep her job in television, says bitterly, "In college, they lied to us twice. They said it would be equal. And they said it would be safe."

The objective facts support these women's fears. MacKinnon cites evidence that more sex discrimination cases are won by men than by women. The experience of Kathy Young is common: Young had witnesses to sexual harassment by her boss, kept notebooks and other evidence, and brought the case to trial.

An Alabama judge ruled that Young couldn't have been sexually harassed, because she did not dye her hair or wear makeup, and in his opinion, her employer's wife was better-looking. The EEOC failed to help her appeal, which Young had to drop when she ran out of money. Her co-workers now tell her that they've learned from her example—they keep their heads down. "The system doesn't work," says Young.

A bright, 29-year-old corporate lawyer made clear to me the reach of this chilling effect: Women lawyers, she said, had been unjustly, disproportionately fired from her firm. "I don't understand," I said. "You're a lawyer. Can't you take legal action?" "You really don't understand," she said grimly. "The legal profession is run by men; it's a company town. If you stick your neck out as a feminist, you get blacklisted."

> *"If they are to be free from harassment . . . , women will need to reinvigorate a sophisticated feminism."*

It is those professional women on the "inside"—with the most to lose—who express the greatest fear of what they describe as the professional suicide of speaking up for one's own rights or beliefs as a woman. This silence is neither apathy nor selfishness nor cowardice. It is silencing by economic pressure in a male-dominated workplace during a worldwide recession. Clearly, the best way you stop a revolution is by giving people something to lose.

Denying Feminist Beliefs

The query—"You're not a feminist, are you?" has been a test oath for women seeking to move ahead: They are asked to leave their gender loyalties at the door. This eviscerates potential collective action by women on the job before it can begin.

The middle-class sisterhood of the 1970s was united in its outsider status; it had everything to gain from forceful feminist behavior. The middle-class ambitious insiders of the 1990s are isolated in a masculine work force, pitted against one another for the few jobs at the top that go to women, and put under pressure to exchange women's rights for career advancement. This gives many women two voices, two realities—one public and male-identified, the other private and true. Each woman must either sit still and be careful not to rock the boat, or fight her fight alone—and probably lose.

Hence the electrifying reaction by women to Hill's allegations; American women have been startled by a manifestation of their own potential collective power. For the one minority that is a majority, the lessons of the Hill-Thomas crisis should be clear already: In the 1990s, if they are to be free from harassment in the workplace and represented in the Senate, women will need to reinvigorate a sophisticated feminism that invests them with the strength of solidarity in the workplace. Only this will make it professionally and personally safe for women to claim in daily life the rights that the EEOC prints for them on paper.

Socialism Would Reduce Sexual Harassment

by *The People*

About the author: The People *is a weekly socialist newspaper.*

Sexual harassment and violence directed at women are partly a product of the historic subordination of women and partly a product of social conditioning that encourages such conduct. But above all, they are products of our present social and economic system, which creates the material conditions and social climate that constantly reproduce and reinforce sexist behavior from one generation to the next. A socialist society would eradicate the underlying material and social causes of such behavior and ultimately put an end to it.

This does not mean that a socialist society would cause sexist harassment and violence to magically and instantly disappear. But it would create conditions that would lead to their eradication. Even prior to the establishment of socialism, the process of building a mass socialist movement—with its raising of class-consciousness and its emphasis on building working-class unity and solidarity—would itself considerably reduce the problem.

Capitalism Promotes Harassment

Capitalism perpetuates the sexist oppression of women, including sexual harassment and violence, in a number of ways.

First of all, as Marx pointed out well over a century ago, capitalism dehumanizes *all* workers, as it alienates them from their work. That is, workers under capitalism are compelled to work for another in order to live, and are divorced from their product; they do not engage in work freely, on their own terms. Thus, workers are alienated from their own human nature as thinking, creative beings, and, as Marx observed, even the "most natural relation" of man to woman is thereby debased.

The commodity status of labor power—the fact that workers must *sell* their

"Question Period," *The People*, July 27, 1991. Reprinted with permission.

life activity to another—and the fact that even sexual relations themselves can take the form of a commodity, add to the dehumanizing character of this system.

Competition and Power

Capitalism is also a system in which workers are forced to compete with one another for limited job and advancement opportunities, in which workers are oppressed on the job, and in which they are taught to vie for positions of *power* over others—material gain and enhanced social status being the rewards of attaining such power. Each of these characteristics of capitalism also contributes to the fostering of sexist conduct.

Job competition is a factor insofar as sexual harassment can be an expression of men seeking to retain their relative advantage in the labor market. For example, a 1981 report on sexual harassment in the Pacific Telephone and Telegraph Company noted that "the overwhelming majority of the incidents" were directed at "women breaking into jobs they once were excluded from."

According to one news report, the director of the Santa Clara County [California] Commission on the Status of Women, which receives 30 to 40 complaints of sexual harassment every month, blames the problem on a "backlash against the women's movement and harsher economic times that have increased competition for jobs."

Sexist attitudes, forged on the job and in the culture at large, are bound to carry over into the home. Economic hardships, including unemployment, and the often humiliating oppression on the job that workers face, are clearly connected to domestic oppression and violence against women. This has been demonstrated both by statistical studies on the effects of unemployment and by the observations of those who have studied domestic violence. Denied power and subjected to stress in their work life, some male workers react by violently asserting their power at home. And in a system that still discriminates against women, women's economic dependence upon men is another factor that can reinforce such abuse.

"Our present social and economic system . . . creates the material conditions and social climate that constantly reproduce and reinforce sexist behavior."

At the same time, in a system that reveres power and regards workers as objects in production, those who *have* obtained positions of power often develop an arrogance that prompts them to use their power for sexual ends. Managers and executives who belittle or abuse women workers, or who make sexual favors a condition for promotion or continued employment, are certainly among the more common perpetrators of sexual harassment.

Of course, sexist attitudes are reproduced by our culture in a number of different ways, from childrearing practices to media messages. And violence against women is to some extent a product of past domestic violence or abuse. But the underlying forces that continue to give new impetus to sexism and violence against women are economic. Above all, the capitalist class materially benefits from the perpetuation of sexist oppression and discrimination.

All of these factors will be eliminated with the establishment of socialism. In a socialist society, the associated producers will collectively be the masters of their own work, their own conditions of work and their own economic fate. There will be no more selling of labor power, no more labor markets, no more competition for jobs, no more unemployment, poverty and economic insecurity. Managers will be responsible to the workers who elect them; the workers will democratically determine the policies governing their workplace and their industry. Thus, there will be no more top-down hierarchy of power and privilege, and no more oppression on the job.

Cultural practices will change, in keeping with a new social atmosphere promoting human dignity and the benefits of cooperation for the social good.

No doubt, there will be residual problems to confront until the poisonous aftereffects of capitalism on human behavior are expunged from society. Accordingly, during the period just after the establishment of socialism, a socialist industrial union government would take whatever common-sense measures are needed to protect the people from aberrant individuals.

Whether or not that would include something akin to a "restraining order" can only be a matter of speculation. What is more certain is that genuine efforts to counsel, educate and rehabilitate the offending individuals would be emphasized. In the social climate created by socialism, those efforts would achieve a high rate of success. In time, the matter will become moot, as socialism overcomes the last vestiges of the oppression of women.

> *"The capitalist class materially benefits from the perpetuation of sexist oppression and discrimination."*

Anti-Harassment Guidelines Would Reduce Sexual Harassment in the Church

by Joy Jordan-Lake

About the author: *Joy Jordan-Lake is the associate pastor of Cambridgeport Baptist Church in Cambridge, Massachusetts, and director of print media for the Greater Boston Baptist Association.*

Maria, a long-time New England resident and evangelical Christian, had tried to convince herself she was imagining things, that surely the fault must be in her perception of the new pastor's conduct and not in his conduct itself—after all, he was a man of God. As an active member and influential leader of Christian education in her Boston-area church, she was determined to give her pastor every benefit of any doubt.

Having accepted a ride home from a Sunday-school teacher's meeting with the clergyman, who lived in the vicinity, Maria was startled when he caught her arm and began caressing it. But she managed to persuade herself that he was merely expressing concern—albeit inappropriately—for the current difficulties in her life. Although she felt uncomfortable enough to retreat promptly into her house, Maria kept the incident to herself.

"I just wouldn't let myself think about it," she says. "I just kept telling myself it was all in my head, that I was making a big deal of nothing."

Other Women Also Harassed

During marriage counseling in which she and her husband were attempting to deal with his violent and angry outbursts, Maria again detected suggestions of

Joy Jordan-Lake, "Conduct Unbecoming a Preacher," *Christianity Today*, February 10, 1992. Used by permission, Christianity Today, 1992.

physical attraction to her on the part of her pastor—behavior she again chose to ignore. But when he called her into his office one Sunday on the pretense of hearing how her classes were progressing and then asked her intensely personal questions about her sex life—claiming that her husband, from whom she was by then separated, wanted to know—Maria began to take her perceptions more seriously. Eventually, she confided in a church elder whom she trusted.

> *"Abuse of pastoral relationships occurs more frequently than the person in the pew would imagine."*

More than a little disturbed, the elder confessed she had previously disregarded similar testimonies from two other women. In all three cases, the women had been particularly vulnerable in the midst of life crises—struggling with broken marital bonds, raising children as single parents, dealing with stress—and had looked to the spiritual leader of their congregation for support, comfort, and guidance. In all three cases, he had betrayed that trust.

Confronting the Unspeakable

In recent years, certain TV evangelists have provided abundant fodder for hungry journalists and stand-up comics. But it is not just the piranhas of pop culture that pay attention. The scandalous exposés of religious figures over the past several years have not been lost on the general public. A Gallup poll taken soon after a spate of well-publicized clergy sex scandals found only 60 percent of adults label the honesty and ethical standards of the clergy as "high" or "very high," a drop from 67 percent in 1985. In a Gallup rating of 25 professions and their publicly perceived ethical standards, the clergy lost its 1985 first-place laurels, now finishing second, a nose behind pharmacists.

Certainly, we read with surprising frequency cases of clergy sexual misconduct. But couldn't such cases merely *seem* surprisingly frequent, highly publicized precisely because they represent an aberration, a blight upon a typically pristine record? How pervasive is inappropriate sexual behavior among clergy?

Research on the issue remains in its nascent stages; only lately have books and articles confronting the formerly unspeakable sin begun to appear. In addition, the conspiracy of silence endemic to both the individuals' and the institutional church's vested interests in protecting reputations conspires against the gathering of hard data. But that, too, is part of the story.

Those who research or work with clergy sexual misconduct differ in their perspectives on its frequency, causes, and proper disciplinary measures. One corporate opinion, however, tallies unanimously: abuse of pastoral relationships occurs more frequently than the person in the pew would imagine.

While conceding that statistically sound studies "have yet to be done," Marie Fortune, executive director of Seattle's Center for the Prevention of Sexual and

Domestic Violence, observes that in a self-reporting survey of therapists, 10 percent of the men and 1 percent of the women admitted having had sexual contact with at least one client. Based on her own study and experience, Fortune suggests that clergy percentages probably fare no better. An ordained United Church of Christ minister, Fortune has served as a consultant in numerous clergy sexual misconduct incidents.

The research of pastoral counselor G. Lloyd Rediger corroborates Fortune's opinion, suggesting in his book *Ministry and Sexuality* that 10 percent of clergy are guilty of sexual malfeasance. Another 15 percent, he believes, are approaching the line of misconduct.

In 1987 *Christianity Today*'s research department surveyed evangelical ministers about pastoral sexual misconduct. The results, published in the Winter 1988 issue of *Leadership Journal*, show that conservative churches are not immune from the problem. When asked, "Since you've been in local-church ministry, have you ever done anything with someone (not your spouse) that you feel was sexually inappropriate?" 23 percent said yes. In response to another question, 12 percent (approximately 1 in 8) admitted to having sexual intercourse with someone other than their spouse.

A 1990 United Methodist study on clergy and laity, *Sexual Harassment in the United Methodist Church*, indicated that of the nearly 1,600 individuals surveyed, nearly 23 percent of laywomen said they had been harassed, 17 percent by their own pastor and 9 percent by another minister. While the United Methodist study's definition of harassment—"any sexually related behavior that is unwelcome, offensive or which fails to respect the rights of others"—is less specific than is desirable, its results elucidate very real, if still shrouded, concerns.

A Generic Male Malady?

Fortune adamantly differentiates between clergy sexual immorality occurring outside congregational boundaries and sexual involvement that abuses the role and invested authority of a pastor or Christian counselor. By way of analogy, she notes that while Jimmy Swaggart's visiting a prostitute evinced "a problem with his own sexuality" and created a dilemma for his church, he "evidently did not betray his pastoral relationship" with any individual congregation members. By contrast, though, "Jim Bakker used his position and power to coerce and manipulate" a woman within his own ministry into sexual involvement. "There's an ethical distinction here most people don't make," she asserts. In the *Christianity Today* survey, over two-thirds of the cases of pastoral sexual misconduct occurred with someone within the pastor's own congregation.

> *"Over two-thirds of the cases of pastoral sexual misconduct occurred with someone within the pastor's own congregation."*

San Francisco psychiatrist Peter Rutter, author of *Sex in the Forbidden Zone*, concurs with Fortune and Rediger on the extent of clergy sexual misconduct and the unique ramifications of professional breach of faith. Examining over 1,000 case studies covering several professions that necessitate the development of "special trust" relationships (i.e., psychiatrists, professors, medical doctors, attorneys, and clergy), Rutter concludes that the results bode no better for religious professionals than for any others, adding, "I found this to be a generic male malady in our culture."

But C. Roy Woodruff, executive director of the American Association of Pastoral Counselors, and Wade Rowatt, associate dean of Southern Baptist Theological Seminary's School of Theology, argue that among ministers, there are fewer cases of sexual misconduct than in corresponding secular communities. Rowatt contends that other professions lack "the moral restrictions" of the ministry and that sexual misconduct professionally remains "not as devastating" to secular careers. Both Rowatt and Woodruff, though, perceive the crisis as occurring unequivocally "too often" and apparently with increased incidence—or at least increased reporting.

> *"To challenge one's actual or perceived superior—professionally, academically, spiritually—has historically been dangerous for women."*

The problem seems to have manifested no preponderance in any one denomination, according to Fortune, nor have the statistics comparing mainline, evangelical, and fundamentalist churches shown notable differences in how often the problem occurs.

And though the Roman Catholic church has received significantly more media attention in regard to priests' illicit sexual conduct, particularly pedophilia, many experts surmise the betrayal of pastoral relationships occurs with a similar frequency in Catholic and Protestant circles.

No Clear Guidelines

Both Fortune and Norris Smith, a consultant with the (Southern) Baptist Sunday School Board, point to a lack of accountability and clear professional guidelines among individual pastors as contributors to ethical misdeeds. Smith, a specialist in the area of forced termination of Southern Baptist pastors, conducted a study revealing "immorality" as a leading cause of their dismissals, second only to "lack or abuse of communication." The survey defined immorality as encompassing "sexual misconduct, substantive lying and the misuse or embezzlement of church funds."

Similarly, a 1984 report by the ecumenical Washington (state) Association of Churches concluded not only that "sexual abuse on the part of pastor and pastoral counselors . . . is more widespread than commonly believed," but also that churches lacked the knowledge and organizational structures to deal with these crises. Responding to the report in his book *Pastoral Ethics*, Yale Divinity School professor Gaylord B. Noyce observes, "The surprise . . . is that the issues must be spelled out at all, since one might have thought that such knowledge and commitments could be assumed."

> *"The onus of responsibility always lies with the pastor in keeping pastoral relationships within moral bounds."*

George Ensworth, clinical director of Charis Psychological Services and professor emeritus in pastoral counseling at Gordon-Conwell Theological Seminary, observes that "pastors, particularly young, highly motivated pastors, who get into trouble [are usually driven by] another issue: need for recognition, affirmation, security. The sexual aspect is secondary," thus allowing it to "sneak up on them."

Acknowledging "it's less a theology issue than a personality issue," Rowatt proposes that the current increase of stress on ministers exacerbates the problem. Under the "corporate model of the church," he explains, "ministers are expected to be corporate heads, performing successfully in evangelism, church growth, pastoral care, social involvement in the community. . . . They're being asked to do jobs they're not trained for," such as too much "in-depth counseling—they get in over their heads."

Inability to compete with glitzy media personalities with whom the congregation compares their pastor may create "such stress" on clergy that they neglect their own families; the minister "doesn't see his or her family deteriorating until it's too late," Rowatt submits. "As stress increases, one's good judgment decreases," Woodruff echoes.

Rutter sees a broader cultural phenomenon of "power imbalance between men and women" contributing to the peril that women, who "in our society are taught to accept exploitation," would not "even realize when their sexual boundaries are being encroached upon." Not until the midseventies, he notes, did women begin to speak out on sexual harassment. To challenge one's actual or perceived superior—professionally, academically, spiritually—has historically been dangerous for women, who may now find it unavoidable. And the corollary is clear: men must learn to shun the seductive "intoxication of power and intimacy."

Not Just an Affair

But whatever the societal backdrop, Fortune is emphatic that this violation of the pastoral role and misuse of authority should never be considered "just an affair" or "just a momentary lapse of judgment." She asserts that those most susceptible to the inherent attraction of a pastor, who seems to encompass compassion, sensitivity, and power, are often already experiencing a life crisis: family death, divorce, illness, physical abuse, incest. When that person is seeking help, a pastor's abusing that trust relationship by stepping—or even allowing him or herself to be coaxed—beyond professional ethical boundaries "involves taking advantage of vulnerability."

> *"Churches should . . . develop clear professional ethical guidelines spelling out the procedures and consequences for sexual misconduct."*

Dispelling misconceptions of "consenting adults," Fortune insists that the onus of responsibility *always* lies with the pastor in keeping pastoral relationships within moral bounds. The dynamics of a pastor-parishioner or counselor-client relationship create a context such that any behavior moving beyond those bounds "takes place in the absence of meaningful consent"—that is, without mutuality, equality, shared power, and a nonpunitive outcome, says Fortune.

Rutter, too, maintains that "the factors of power, trust, and dependency" render the professional consistently responsible for "the seen or unseen dependency elements that ultimately develop" despite any "level of provocation or apparent consent" on the part of the parishioner. Woodruff likens the dynamics of clergy sexual misconduct, particularly in counseling, to those of an incestuous relationship, both containing "the ingredients of authority, care and nurture," which, if abused, are "ultimately devastating."

In some cases, however, Fortune would attest that a pastor not only knew better, but consciously capitalized on that position. In her book *Is Nothing Sacred?* Fortune records her work as a consultant and advocate for six women who had been sexually involved, unbeknownst to each other, with their charismatic, successful, young pastor. One, an older woman, had gone to him seeking counseling upon the death of her husband of many years. Another, quite young, sought comfort and guidance from the shepherd of the local flock—and was raped by him. All were verbally and emotionally harassed. Subsequent investigation suggested the involvement of many more women who chose to remain silent.

Of these more rare "prima donna types" Woodruff observes, "They lose a sense of their own boundaries, develop a messianic sense of themselves. They convince a woman 'it's okay, because I'm a man of God.'" Ethically and morally, he adds, they cease to "differentiate between themselves and God."

An Ounce of Prevention

Whatever the circumstances of a publicly known clergy ethics violation, "the congregation is also a victim of the offense," the Washington Association of Churches' report asserts, recommending the aid of "a trained resource person who can assist . . . in the healing process so that the congregation can work through the pain of this trauma and begin to carry on its mission."

Fortune, however, reports the institutional church's propensity to "protect itself by preventing disclosure of professional misconduct," often at the expense of other victims. Initially concerned with maintaining its own image of integrity, she writes that the church may prefer "to shoot the messenger, that is, to denigrate whoever had the courage to tell the secret." Often reacting too much "like a family upon the revelation of incest," a congregation may initially attempt denial or coverup, resulting ultimately in undermining its credibility and exacerbating harm to those involved.

Early Harassment Problems

The widely publicized involvement of renowned preacher and pastor of Plymouth Church in Brooklyn Heights, New York, Henry Ward Beecher (1813-87) with Elizabeth Tilton, Beecher's parishioner and wife of his close friend, provides a classic example of this phenomenon. It began in 1868 with pastoral calls consoling Tilton on the death of her child. Four years later, rumors were flying, and by 1875, Elizabeth's husband, Theodore, had brought litigation against Beecher. In the face of overwhelming evidence, the congregation completely exonerated their pastor. In 1878, all those testifying against Beecher were excommunicated, including Elizabeth Tilton, who died 19 years later, alienated, ostracized, alone.

Sometimes ecclesiastical mishandling of such cases may entail significant financial expenditures. Over the next ten years, for instance, the Roman Catholic church will pay approximately one billion dollars in civil lawsuits for "alleged sexual misconduct on the part of its clergy," Fortune notes. "A lawsuit is the last resort for most people," she believes, unnecessary "if church bodies would deal with it and provide . . . justice, clear acknowledgment of what happened and disciplinary action toward the offender." If nothing else, she adds wryly, it makes "good economic sense."

Preventing Harassment in Churches

Churches on both ends of the theological spectrum handle such a tragedy ineptly, says Fortune. In her experience, conservative congregations demonstrate a proclivity for "rallying to support 'the poor brother who's fallen from grace,'" accompanied by "no attention whatsoever to the victims."

On the more liberal end, churches that may espouse a "more open attitude toward sexuality" manifest a "tendency for not wanting to deal

> *"Churches should encourage mutually supportive clergy marriages."*

with it at all." Experts agree that disciplinary action and the offender's prospect for rehabilitation vary widely according to the nature and circumstances of the offense.

But the most efficacious approach is clearly to work at prevention. Churches should encourage mutually supportive clergy marriages; develop clear professional ethical guidelines spelling out the procedures and consequences for sexual misconduct; set limits on time, place, and circumstances of pastoral visits and counseling sessions; decrease pastoral stress factors (i.e., limit time and job demands for the pastor); and put into place ministerial accountability (to the congregation, to denominational officials, and, primarily, to God).

"Our theology," concludes Fortune, "is more than adequate to guide our response."

Chapter 4

Can Broad Legal Definitions of Sexual Harassment Be Effectively Used in the Courts?

Sexual Harassment in the Courts: An Overview

by Nancy Gibbs et al.

About the author: *Nancy Gibbs is an associate editor for* Time, *a weekly newsmagazine.*

America set about smashing china and moving furniture around in the household of its public morality, with the knowledge that before it was all over no one would know where to find anything anymore. Conversation became suddenly careful; the pinups were peeled off the wall. The issue of sexual harassment—what it is, why it happens, who's to blame—was a fascinating topic to obsess upon as a nation, wonder about in private, argue about in public. It was also a long, bruising week of bumping into issues that many of us didn't know were there.

In America's workplaces, men and women reintroduced themselves with a suspicion that their relationships had changed forever. Men who have worked closely with women for years asked them flat out, "Have you ever felt threatened or insulted or offended by anything I've said or done?" Many women privately shared their experiences and their anger, for the first time taking seriously behavior they had long taken for granted. Some of them, wary of being cast as victims, wondered whether in the end all the sudden attention to the issue would do them more harm than good.

The issue of sexual harassment ricochets off other crucial debates this country has yet to resolve about the boundaries of morality and law. The boss who kept his employees' menstrual cycles marked on a wall calendar was, by any measure, a lout. Was he a criminal? How useful is it to establish a category of behavior that runs the gamut from rudeness to rape? Should it be embedded in the law that men and women react differently to the same comments and behavior?

The questions and conversations were all the more pointed because, despite the clarity of the legal language, sexual harassment is a complex issue, its incidence difficult to measure. It is uniformly cast as a gender issue, since the overwhelming majority of cases involve female workers being harassed by male colleagues and supervisors. But when pollsters ask women whether they have ever been targets of harassment, the answers depend on how the question is phrased, which helps explain why some surveys find that 90% of women view themselves as victims and others find less than half that number.

> *"Despite the clarity of the legal language, sexual harassment is a complex issue."*

As last week's crash course made clear, most women and men, especially most Senators, had only the barest understanding of the power of the law. Under Equal Employment Opportunity Commission guidelines issued in 1980 and unanimously affirmed by the Supreme Court in 1986, sexual harassment includes not just physical but also verbal and "environmental" abuse. Under the law, there are two broadly recognized forms. The first involves a "quid pro quo" in which a worker is compelled to trade sex for professional survival. In 1986 an Ohio woman won a $3.1 million verdict against an employer who invited her to perform oral sex or lose her job.

The other part of the law refers to a "hostile working environment," and it is here that the debates get most heated. The phrase covers any unwelcome sexual behavior that makes it hard for a worker to do her job or that creates a hostile or offensive environment. Charles Looney, regional director of the EEOC New England office in Boston, says the courts are more concerned with the woman's reaction than the man's intent. "If I run a stop sign, I have broken the law even if I did not intend to," he says. "People can create hostile environments without knowing that it would be considered sexual harassment, but they are still liable."

The courts may have worked it all out, but most Americans have not. As people . . . wrestled with the ambiguous definitions of sexual harassment, many were left with a conviction that, as with pornography, they know it when they see it. The ugly realities of many American workplaces give the legal language its vividness. There is, for instance, the case of Edith Magee, who worked a shovel and drove a dump truck for the St. Paul, Minn., sewage department. "There was always this implied threat that if they didn't like you, they would use their authority to get you in trouble," she says of her supervisors. Her employer settled her case for $75,000 but denied any wrongdoing. "I knew when I walked into the lunchroom and my boss was reading *Hustler*, it was going to be bad," she says. "He'd show me pictures of dildoes and say, 'Is your husband's this big?' There was no way you could push him away. He would just go and go and never stop. The idea was, if you were a female and did something as low-class as shovel, then you deserved what you got."

Such stories, echoed a thousand, a hundred thousand times, helped lawyers explain that sexual harassment is not about civility. It is not about a man making an unwelcome pass, telling a dirty joke or commenting on someone's appearance. Rather it is an abuse of power in which a worker who depends for her livelihood and professional survival on the goodwill of a superior is made to feel vulnerable. "This is not automatically a male-female issue," says Wendy Reid Crisp, the director of the National Association for Female Executives, the largest women's professional association in the country. "We define this issue as economic intimidation."

Edith Magee is typical in that the most common targets of harassment in blue-collar jobs tend to be women who are breaking into fields once dominated by men. In white-collar professions, most victims are "women in lowly positions," says Susan Rubenstein, an attorney in San Francisco who specializes in sexual-harassment cases. "A secretary will get harassed before a lawyer, a paralegal will get harassed before an associate." Particularly in male bastions, women find that feminism becomes, ironically, a weapon in the attack.

"It's not just some guy grabbing you and pushing you in a closet and saying, 'If you don't let me fondle you, I'm going to fire you,'" explains Susan Faludi, author of a new book, *Backlash: The Undeclared War Against American Women.* "It's more the subtler form of making women uncomfortable by turning the workplace into a locker room and then telling them, 'What's the matter, you can't handle it? You wanted equality; I'm going to give it to you with a vengeance.' "

> *"When pollsters ask women whether they have ever been targets of harassment, the answers depend on how the question is phrased."*

Faludi cites the case of Diane Joyce, who fought for 17 years to become the first female skilled crafts worker in the history of Santa Clara, Calif. The real fight began after she finally started the job. When the roadmen trained Joyce to drive the bobtail trucks, says Faludi, they kept changing instructions; one gave her driving tips that nearly blew up the engine. She had to file a formal grievance just to get the pair of coveralls that she said were withheld from her. In the yard the men kept the ladies' room locked, and on the road they wouldn't stop to let her use a bathroom. "You wanted a man's job, you learn to pee like a man," she recalls a superior telling her. "She is not talking about being attacked in the office," says Faludi. "It's a slow, relentless accumulation of slights and insults that add up to the same thing—the message that we don't want you here and we are going to make your hours here uncomfortable." In the years since women were integrated into the armed forces, that once all-male preserve has struggled to counter the macho image that long prevailed. SEXUAL HARASSMENT IS NOT FROWNED ON HERE; IT'S GRADED was one sign, now removed, in the Pentagon. By and large, the military has succeeded in impressing officers with the importance of the issue, though enlisted men are not always as enlightened. But there is one big exception, according to Linda Grant De Pauw, president of the Minerva Center, an educational facility dealing with women in the armed services. "The absolute military ban on homosexuals creates an opening for sexual harassment," she says. "Military women live in mortal fear of being called a dyke. When the man says, 'Sleep with me or I'll say you're a lesbian,' it is terrifically effective where women know they may be kicked out if the charge is made."

Defining unwelcome or offensive advances sounds like a subjective judgment; many people were . . . worried that sexual harassment is anything an accuser says it is. But in a landmark ruling, the Ninth U.S. Circuit Court in California ruled that the law covers any remark or behavior that a "reasonable woman" would find to be a problem—and acknowledged that a woman's perception might differ from a man's. Judge Robert Beezer wrote that "conduct that many men consider unobjectionable may offend many women." He noted that because women are much more likely to be victims of rape and sexual assault, they have a "stronger incentive to be concerned with sexual behavior." Men, in addition, are more likely to view sexual conduct as harmless.

Underneath that reasoning is the notion that there is a continuum running from the innocent gesture to the brutal assault. It is an interpretation fused to an ideology that places all behavior in the context of male power. In the view of Boston University psychology professor Frances Grossman, "From the guys who wink on the street to the biology professor who tells a sexist joke in class, to the guy who says, 'Hey, baby, let's go out,' to the guy who rapes—all are of a piece in their role of disempowering women. Men say these are not related behaviors. Flirting and jokes are fine, and rape is bad, they say. But increasingly, sociologists say they all send the same disempowering message to women."

That line of argument brings shouts of anger not only from men who feel maligned but also from women who feel belittled. They argue that women do themselves and their careers no favor when they play victim or perpetuate an unhealthy culture of self-pity by asking to be coddled and protected from rudeness and boorish behavior. Sexual harassment is not about sex; it is about power, the reasoning goes, and if women act powerless at work, they will almost certainly be taken advantage of.

> *"It's not just some guy grabbing you and pushing you in a closet and saying, 'If you don't let me fondle you, I'm going to fire you.' "*

Here is a rare intersection between the opinions of some ardent feminists and some profound antifeminists. "If a girl can survive high school, she ought to be able to deal with the office," says Phyllis Schlafly, a longtime crusader against feminist causes. For Schlafly, the sexual-harassment argument is a perfect example of how "feminists are asking to have it both ways." Says she: "They have spent 20 years preaching that there isn't any difference between men and women, and now they want to turn around and claim sexual harassment if somebody says something that they don't like." The very issue is patronizing, says Schlafly, because it implies that women cannot handle uncomfortable situations without the help of government.

> *"The law covers any remark or behavior that a 'reasonable woman' would find to be a problem."*

This is not just the view of an extremist. Scholars such as Ellen Frankel Paul, deputy director of the Social Philosophy and Policy Center at Bowling Green State University in Ohio, argue that the courts are a dangerous mechanism for policing behavior. "Do we really want legislators and judges delving into our most intimate private lives," she asks, "deciding when a look is a leer and when a leer is a civil rights offense? Should people have a legally enforceable right not to be offended by others? At some point, the price for such protection is the loss of both liberty and privacy rights."

From this perspective, women have a lot to lose if they press the issue of sexual harassment too far. Particularly in white-collar settings, younger workers rely on mentors to help them learn the ropes and advance their careers. If a boss is afraid that his interest in a protégé's success will be misconstrued, the safer path is to avoid mentor relationships. "While it is perfectly fine—and normal—for a mentor to say to a man, 'Let's have a drink, or play golf, and talk about that promotion,' it's harder for a mentor to do that with a woman outside strict business hours without incurring some legal risk," notes Terry Morehead Dworkin, a business-law professor at Indiana University. One solution, of course, is for more women to be in the position to promote younger women, but in many corporations that day is still far off.

Some men were also impatient with the way the issue has been cast. Though his view is hardly typical, Fredric Hayward, the executive director of Men's Rights Inc. in Sacramento, examines the exact same situations but finds a different victim. Men may wield professional power, he says, but women have sexual power. "If I or a woman does not get a job because a female competitor displays more enticing cleavage, then what are we victims of?" he asks. "If I or a woman does not get a promotion because a female competitor has an affair with our boss, then what are we victims of?" In his view, men and women have an equal incentive to abuse whatever power they have. "For every executive who chases an executive around the desk," he declares, "there is a secretary who dreams of marrying an executive and not having to be a secretary anymore."

There are many possible answers to Hayward's characterization of women's professional behavior, which points to the dangers of generalization on this issue. One rebuttal might come from all the women who have struggled to erase their gender at the office door. "The minute I get in, I become one of the guys," says stand-up comic Reno, who works in comedy clubs. "I've got to take my breasts off and talk from the head up and slap everybody around. I become this desexualized creature so that we can all work together."

Susan Webb runs a consulting firm in Seattle that helps companies educate their employees about the issue of harassment. She says men almost always greet her with derision. "So now we're going to find out how to do it" is one reaction. Or, "I've been trying for years to get someone to sexually harass me." Says Webb: "The laughing is not because they are mean or bad, but because they really don't understand it." Part of what fuels the initial jokes, says Webb, is the fear of being blamed for or embarrassed about sexual harassment.

Many male supervisors are now wondering how careful they will have to be with their humor, their off-hand remarks, their courtship of colleagues in whom they are romantically interested. Florida state representative Kathy Chinoy is a lawyer whose specialty is sexual harassment. She finds that many of her colleagues in the statehouse are genuinely bewildered by the issue, though younger men, who grew up with a different code of conduct, seem to have a more acute understanding. She recommends a simple litmus test for men who are seeking guidance on what is appropriate and what is not: "Would you want your mother, sister or daughter exposed to that?"

> *"Many male supervisors are now wondering how careful they will have to be with their humor."*

The confusion can cut both ways. For a woman who is attracted to her superior, the inferences that colleagues may draw from that relationship make her think long and hard before entering into a romance. Is it worth it for me to date my boss, a woman may think, if in the future others will snicker that my success has come about not because of my talent but because I'm involved with my supervisor?

How can it be, many people wondered, . . . that such a huge majority of women seem to have had some visceral and personal experience with this issue and yet so few cases ever end up being formally settled, by the employer or by the court? Those who charge that the issue is exaggerated point to the tiny number of sexual-harassment charges—5,557 complaints—that ended up before the Equal Employment Opportunity Commission last year. It is true that cases are also handled in private litigation, but overall the number of formal complaints reflects a minuscule fraction of the number of women who say they have experienced harassment at work.

But the fact that there is a wide gap between what women say they experience and what they take to court sheds considerable light on the issue. Lawyers are loath to take such cases, because the risks are great and the rewards small. The burden of proof is very high; as the Eighth Circuit Court of Appeals in St. Louis noted in one ruling, the laws on sexual harassment "do not mandate an employment environment worthy of a Victorian salon." When women were asked why they had never taken formal action, the answer was stunningly consistent: Why commit professional suicide?

Though Anita Hill brought the issue into the spotlight, she was preceded by another highly visible, impressive and articulate woman who helped shape the national debate. When Stanford University neurosurgeon Frances Conley resigned her post . . . to protest the behavior of her male colleagues, she forced men and women to weigh the costs of taking complaints public. Conley made a useful lightning rod, since by her demeanor she dispelled the notion of accusers as crybabies or oversensitive types who are not sophisticated enough to cope with office banter. She announced . . . that she would rejoin the faculty, having been persuaded that her message had been heard. . . .

But for women with less of a pulpit, the results of coming forward can be devastating. Simone Lochlear, a 28-year-old restaurant manager in the South, filed a sexual-harassment suit against the manager of Washington's Dubliner Restaurant and Pub, who she alleged twice asked her to perform oral sex in front of another employee. After she filed a claim at the District of Columbia's human-rights office, she says, the manager had a private detective follow her and take notes on how she worked. She was fired two months later for failing to ring up drinks correctly. Her employer denies her charge, and she is still awaiting a ruling on her case. "It makes me really angry that someone could do this to me and mess with my mind. I was standing up for what was right and became the victim."

For many women the decision about whether to take any action or lodge a complaint is an economic one. Any action that might lead to loss of a job, or even alienation from co-workers, may seem too costly even for one's dignity or peace of mind. Anita Allen, a black woman who grew up in the South, became a philosophy professor at Carnegie-Mellon and went on to become a Wall Street lawyer. . . . She taught at Harvard law school as a visiting professor. "I have experienced sexual harassment in every area that I have worked, from comments to innuendo to times when I have literally been chased around a desk," she says. "I have accepted jobs from people who engaged in sexual harassment because I needed the job. I never considered a legal suit. I tried to pretend it didn't happen. Today I'd be different."

"The fact that there is a wide gap between what women say they experience and what they take to court sheds considerable light on the issue."

The financial cost is often high as well. The only time the EEOC provides free legal help is when it chooses to take the case to court—a rare occurrence. Women must typically hire private litigators, many of whom demand high fees because the cases are so hard to win and the settlements so low. Under the Civil Rights Act of 1964, a woman who wins a suit is entitled to reinstatement with back pay. There is no provision for punitive damages, though some state and municipal laws are more generous. The civil rights bill that is now pending would allow for punitive damages, but President Bush has promised a veto.

> *"For many women the decision about whether to take any action or lodge a complaint is an economic one."*

In the absence of any strong federal enforcement, the responsibility for addressing the issue has fallen to private employers. Their interest in the problem is self-interest: the courts have ruled that companies are liable for their employees' behavior, even if they are unaware of it and have anti-harassment policies in place. According to a 1988 survey of FORTUNE 500 companies by *Working Woman* magazine, ignoring the issue costs a typical FORTUNE 500 company as much as $6.7 million a year in absenteeism, turnover and lost productivity. Three-quarters of the firms have established anti-harassment policies, 90% have received complaints, and 64% acknowledge that most of the complaints they hear are valid. In roughly 80% of cases, the harasser is reprimanded; in 20%, a firing results.

But whatever standards and expectations were in place, . . . they now lie in pieces on the office or the factory floor. Too many conversations occurred, too many stories were told, for men and women to return comfortably to old patterns of behavior. In the immediate future, progress may come on tiptoe. For a little while at least, an excess of care, though dampening the easy working relationships both men and women value, may be an appropriate antidote to so many years of clumsiness and indifference to this issue. Once the ground settles under everyone's feet, perhaps the intricacies of the law will become less important, because the standards of acceptable behavior will have been forever raised.

Broad Legal Definitions Have Been Successfully Used in the Courts

by Susan L. Webb

About the author: *Susan L. Webb is president of Pacific Resource Development Group, Inc., a Seattle-based consulting firm specializing in human relations issues. She is also the editor of the* Webb Report, *a national newsletter on sexual harassment, and is the author of* Step Forward: Sexual Harassment in the Workplace, *from which this viewpoint was taken.*

A few years ago, a pertinent story appeared in the "Slice of Life" column of my local newspaper. ("Slice of Life" is where amusing, silly, or funny little stories are reported for everyone's daily amusement.) In this story, the woman, who worked for a rapid transit authority as a token clerk, claimed that she was subjected to continuous and repeated sexual comments by the general public because of an advertising poster that was behind her work station.

Pushing the Limits

The poster advertised a health club with the caption "Have we got two great figures for you!" The first great figure was the $19.95 they charged to join the club, and the second was "Miss Pin-Up of 1983," lying on her side in a very small string bikini.

When I read the story, I, like most people, thought it was amusing and a little trivial, and I couldn't help thinking that some people—like this woman—really push the limits, that we were getting to the point where everything in the world is considered sexual harassment.

A few months later I heard another interesting story, this one about a pizza parlor whose employees had to wear animal costumes for the entertainment of their young customers. One table cleaner, who dressed like a squirrel, found some holes in her squirrel costume in what she thought were rather embarrassing places, so she took the outfit to her supervisor to get it repaired. Instead of having the uniform fixed, he began teasing her about boy squirrels and girl squirrels, saying he thought that the holes were in "squirrel-appropriate loca-

tions." The final straw for the employee was when her supervisor came up behind her and pantomimed what a boy squirrel would do to a girl squirrel if she had a hole in that particular spot. The person who told me this story was the squirrel's attorney, at a party.

> *"One early survey . . . said that the real problem was not in defining sexual harassment but in recognizing when it occurs."*

Again, I had those same doubting thoughts: the things people do to each other at work are a constant source of amazement, but an attorney! Had we gone too far again? Do we really need an attorney involved in a case like this?

A third story was about a young woman who went into her boss's office one afternoon to pick up an adding machine. Her boss was sitting at his desk, talking with a male employee who was standing across the desk from him. The woman walked around behind her boss's desk and bent over to pick up the machine. Her boss turned around in his swivel chair, to find her rump right in front of his face. The personnel director of this company told me that, without thinking, on the spur of the moment, with no malicious intent whatsoever, the boss "bit the woman on the butt."

Stopping to Think

If you're like most people, by now you're either shaking your head at these stories or smiling or laughing outright. But when people stop to think about harassment instead of just reacting, or when it happens to someone they're close to, like their wife or daughter, husband or son, then the situation changes.

Let's go back through those three stories, starting with the token clerk. If we assume that only twenty thousand people went through her work station on a daily basis and that only one of every hundred made some kind of sexual comment, that's two hundred comments in an eight-hour shift. Even if we assume that only one out of every two hundred made a comment, we're still talking about a hundred comments every single day. You can imagine how tired of that poster the woman was by noon of the first day, or how tired of it her husband was on the second evening, when he'd heard about nothing else for two days. The story's not quite so funny the second time around.

As for the table cleaner in the pizza parlor, it turns out that it wasn't she who had hired the attorney, but her mommy and daddy. The little squirrel was only fifteen years old, and her parents didn't think it was one bit funny when her twenty-two-year-old supervisor pantomimed boy squirrels and girl squirrels behind the counter at ten o'clock at night, when it was just the two of them alone in the store. Not so funny when you think it might be your daughter, grand-daughter, or niece.

And the woman who was bitten didn't complain to anyone because she didn't want to get her boss in trouble; in fact, they were friends. But three weeks later she went to the human resources office and quit. When the personnel director tried to find out why she was leaving, she started crying and told him the story. It seems that the man who witnessed the biting went out and told everyone in the warehouse what he'd seen and how funny it was. Since then, people the woman didn't know had been coming up to her and teasing her about teeth marks or bruises on her behind; people would laugh and giggle when she walked into the lunchroom; some had even asked to see the "tattoo on [her] ass." So she wasn't going to cause problems for anyone. She was embarrassed and very uncomfortable, and she'd decided just to leave. This funny, stupid story just doesn't seem so funny after all, does it?

Recognizing Harassment

One early survey, published in 1981 in the *Harvard Business Review*, said that the real problem was not in defining sexual harassment but in recognizing it when it occurs. The results showed that men and women see sexual harassment very differently. Of course, now, with hindsight, that doesn't seem very surprising, but what it means is that if sexual harassment occurred right in front of us, many of the women would call it harassment and many of the men would call it a joke. And it's not even that simple, because opinions about what is and isn't harassment vary not just between men and women, but between men and men, and women and women.

> *"The behavior in question has to be sexual in nature or sex-based."*

Most often, people think of sexual harassment in two extremes. Many think that the only time it's sexual harassment is when a supervisor or manager says, "Sleep with me or you're fired." Of course that is sexual harassment—the most serious kind—but that is only the tip of the iceberg. At the other extreme are people who think or say that everything in the world is sexual harassment, and if you say "Hi, hon, how's it going?" that's sexual harassment and a suit could be filed against you. That's a slight exaggeration too.

We can think of sexual harassment in two different ways. First, there's what we call the behavioral definition: a common-sense, everyday way of looking at the problem. Second is what we'll call the legal definition: what the EEOC [Equal Employment Opportunity Commission] Guidelines and the courts define as illegal discrimination.

The most common behavioral definition of sexual harassment is "deliberate and/or repeated sexual or sex-based behavior that is not welcome, not asked for, and not returned." There are three major elements and two qualifiers in this definition.

First of all, for it to be sexual harassment, *the behavior in question has to be sexual in nature or sex-based.* In other words, it's behavior with some sort of sexual connotation to it or behavior that occurs because of the victim's being male or female.

The range of behavior with sexual connotations is very wide, and the behavior doesn't necessarily mean that the perpetrator has the intent of having sex. We must think in terms of a continuum of sexual behavior, ranging from the least severe end—including joking, innuendoes, flirting, asking someone for a date—to the most serious end—forced fondling, attempted or actual rape, sexual assault.

As for sex-based behavior—occurring on account of sex or gender—it too can be light or severe. It is negative behavior that is directed at, or has an impact on, only one gender. Negative gender-related behavior can include men putting down the women or women making negative remarks about the men—in other words, a serious battle of the sexes at the job site. . . .

Deliberate and Repeated

Second, *the behavior has to be deliberate and/or repeated.* Some forms of sexual behavior are so graphic and offensive that the first time they occur they are considered deliberate, inappropriate, and sometimes even illegal actions. There are other forms of behavior that must be repeated over and over again before they become harassment. Both are serious and damaging, but we tend to disagree over their being labeled "sexual harassment."

Most of us would agree that such severe sexual behavior as forced fondling, attempted rape, and serious sexual slurs definitely is not permissible. Where we have the difficulty and disagreement is at the other end of the continuum. What one person takes as joking another finds offensive and degrading.

Keep in mind that even comments made in a joking manner may not be bothersome the first few times, but day after day, joke after joke, they cease to be funny or amusing to the person who's receiving them. While the behavior may not be considered illegal sexual harassment, it still has a negative and damaging impact on the employee subjected to it.

> *"What one person takes as joking another finds offensive and degrading."*

One way of looking at it is to remember that *the more severe the behavior is, the fewer times it needs to be repeated before reasonable people define it as harassment; the less severe it is, the more times it needs to be repeated.* This is one of the two qualifiers of the definition. The severity of the behavior must be considered in conjunction with the number of repetitions.

The third part of the definition is that *sexual harassment is not welcome, not asked for, and not returned.* We are not talking about mutual behavior that people engage in together or enjoy. What two people do that is mutual is simply that, mutual, and is usually permissible so long as it doesn't interfere with their work or create a hostile or offensive work environment for others. (I say *usually* because some mutual behavior that may not be defined as harassment—because it *is* mutual—nevertheless still is not permissible in the work environment: mutual buttocks grabbing, mutual graphic sexual jokes, etc.)

> *"Studies have shown that light harassment tends to get worse and become severe when it is not addressed and stopped."*

When considering the welcomeness of the behavior, some people try to place the sole responsibility for setting limits on the victim: "It's not sexual harassment unless she or he says so." That's not quite right.

A Continuum of Behavior

If we go back to the sexual-behavior continuum, we can add the second qualifier: *the less severe the behavior is, the more responsibility the receiver has to speak up* (because some people like this kind of behavior); *the more severe it is, the less responsibility the receiver has to speak up* (the initiator of the behavior should be sensitive enough in the first place to know that it is inappropriate).

The three elements—sexual or sex-based, deliberate and/or repeated, and not welcome, asked for, or returned—along with the two qualifiers of varying degrees of repetition and varying responsibilities of the sender and receiver, make up a complete, and some say too broad, definition of sexual harassment. It is primarily those with a legal perspective who initially feel that this definition may cover too much.

This definition covers more than what a purely legal definition might. The point is that studies have shown that light harassment tends to get worse and become severe when it is not addressed and stopped. By including in your assessment a definition of harassment that includes light, moderate, and severe, you can resolve the situation now and, it is to be hoped, in the future as well. . . .

Power and Harassment

It's also important to remember that sexual harassment is really about power. The harasser either thinks or knows, consciously or unconsciously, that he or she has more power than the harassee. If not, there would be no harassment— the harassee could turn to the harasser and demand that it stop and there would be no issue.

When asked why they file lawsuits or formal complaints outside their organizations—why they did not solve the problem in-house—victims of harassment give two reasons:

- "I didn't think anyone would take me seriously." This says that they felt powerless. They thought or knew that others would laugh or tell them they were being too sensitive.
- "I couldn't get it stopped any other way." This indicates that they were powerless to stop unwanted behavior.

To determine whether behavior should be labeled sexual harassment, first compare it with the behavioral definition: deliberate and/or repeated sexual or sex-based behavior that is not welcome, not asked for, and not returned. Do this analysis for each incident or act, then consider the overall picture.

Sexual Behavior

1. Was the behavior sexual (about sex) or sex-based (on account of sex or directed to or affecting only one sex or gender)? First, plot each occurrence on the continuum so you have some picture of its severity:

- Potentially harassing behavior has the potential to be sexual harassment, particularly if repeated enough times, but it can also be socially acceptable in certain situations. This behavior is more likely to be called inappropriate or out of line, but not truly harassment, especially if just one instance has occurred.

> *"Sexual harassment is really about power."*

- Subtle sexual behavior is sometimes socially acceptable, but some reasonable men and women would see it as offensive and want it stopped. The receivers usually don't want anything done to the sender at this point, other than making him or her stop. The behavior is bothersome, worth mentioning, but would not warrant a formal complaint if it were all that occurred.
- Moderate sexual behavior is not socially acceptable, and reasonable men and women see it as offensive and would want it stopped. The behavior is serious enough that some action must be taken against the sender (such as warning letters or reprimands), in addition to having him or her stop the behavior. The behavior is offensive and could warrant a complaint even if it were all that occurred.
- Severe sexual behavior is never socially acceptable and is so graphic or severe that one instance can call for serious disciplinary action, such as probation, suspension, or termination of the offending employee(s). Included in this category is physical behavior such as attempted or actual rape or sexual assault and verbal behavior such as serious sexual slurs.

2. Was the behavior deliberate and/or repeated? If it was not deliberate—truly accidental—then you most likely cannot label it harassment at all. If it was not accidental, then how often was it repeated? Remember the qualifier: the less se-

131

vere the behavior, the more repetitions required to label it harassment; the more severe, the fewer repetitions needed. Also keep in mind that repeated instances of similar behavior can constitute repetitions: three different sexual remarks could be the same as three repetitions of one comment.

3. Was the behavior welcome, asked for, or returned? Again, remember the qualifier: the less severe the behavior, the more the responsibility of the receiver to speak up; the more severe, the less responsibility the receiver has to speak up and the more responsibility the sender has to monitor his or her own behavior. Did the receiver tell or indicate to the sender that the behavior was unwelcome? Was it necessary that the receiver give notice, or should the sender have known better in the first place?

If the behavior was reciprocated in any way, was there a balance between the seriousness of the sender's behavior and the receiver's response? One of the arguments you will hear is that the complainant employee liked the behavior, engaged in it himself or herself, asked for it, encouraged it, etc. If this is the case, then both (or all) of the parties should be talked to so that this type of behavior is stopped (though it is not to be labeled sexual harassment, since it was welcome). However, first determine whether there was a balance between the sender's behavior and the receiver's response. . . .

EEOC Guidelines and the Courts

The second step in determining whether sexual harassment has occurred is to consider each behavior, then the overall picture, in light of the EEOC Guidelines. There are several key points of the Guidelines that need to be considered. These key points plus court decisions provide the legal definition of sexual harassment and spell out the rights and responsibilities of employers and employees. State laws may also pertain.

1. Section A of the Guidelines says that unwelcome sexual advances, requests for sexual favors, and other verbal or physical conduct of a sexual nature constitutes sexual harassment under any of four conditions:

• When such behavior is either explicitly or implicitly part of a manager's or supervisor's decision to hire or fire someone. When submitting to sexual conduct is a term or condition of employment, it is illegal, whether the request or demand was made outright or simply

> *"The damage caused by the sexual behavior does not have to be a tangible economic consequence such as losing the job or promotion."*

implied. Showing that such a request was implied might involve looking at employment records before and after the request was rejected. When an action amounts to the same thing as an explicit request, it too is illegal.

• When such behavior is used to make other employment decisions such as pay, promotion, or job assignment. Any time an employment decision is based on whether an employee submitted or refused to submit to some form of sexual conduct, it is illegal. The employment decision does not have to actually cost the employee his or her job, nor does the sexual conduct have to be an actual request for sex. The supervisor who plays favorites with workers who go along with his habit of telling dirty jokes or making sexual comments and bends the rules in their favor is making employment decisions based on willingness to submit to sexual conduct.

Quid Pro Quo Harassment

These two conditions are what courts have called quid pro quo harassment: someone with the power to do so, usually a supervisor or manager, offers some kind of tangible job benefit for submission to sexual harassment. In these cases courts have held the employer strictly liable—responsible even when the employer did not know the harassment was occurring and even if it had a policy forbidding such behavior.

- When such behavior has the purpose or effect of unreasonably interfering with the employee's work performance.
- When such behavior creates an intimidating, hostile, or offensive work environment.

Courts have called these two conditions hostile environment harassment: the damage caused by the sexual behavior does not have to be a tangible economic consequence such as losing the job or promotion, but the atmosphere at work becomes so negative that it affects the employee's ability to do his or her job. The sexual behavior is illegal harassment.

The EEOC included the words *purpose or effect* to indicate that intent to harm is not a necessary element of sexual harassment. If an employee's unwanted sexual behavior has the effect of creating a hostile work environment and interfering with another employee's work performance, the first employee's intent may be irrelevant.

To fit the EEOC's definition, sexual harassment must have two characteristics: it is unwelcome and unwanted and it has an impact on an employee's job or work environment. Whether the sexual behavior is directed to an employee face-to-face or

> *"The employer may be held responsible for sexual harassment of its employees by people who are nonemployees."*

behind his or her back, and whether the behavior occurs during breaks or in locker rooms, may not be important so long as it has an impact on the employee's work environment.

2. Section B says that each claim of sexual harassment should be examined on a case-by-case basis. Consideration should be given to the context in which

the behavior took place, the nature of the sexual behavior, and the record as a whole.

3. Sections C and D have to do with the employer's liability. Section C says that the employer may be held "strictly liable" for harassment by supervisors—meaning even when the employer is not aware of the harassment and even when there is a policy forbidding such behavior. Section D says that the employer is liable for co-worker harassment when the employer knows of the harassment and fails to take immediate and appropriate action.

Liability for Harassment

Several courts ruled in 1983 that "strict liability" applies only in quid pro quo harassment cases, in which a tangible job benefit was affected, and the victim can file a charge without notifying management of the harassment. If it is hostile environment harassment, the victim must allow the employer the opportunity to take appropriate action before the victim can file a complaint. This issue is still being addressed by the courts.

4. Section E says that the employer may be held responsible for sexual harassment of its employees by people who are nonemployees—such as customers or the general public—when the employer knows about the harassment and does nothing. In these cases the extent of the employer's control over the situation is examined closely, and if in any way the employer can stop the harassment, it is responsible for doing so.

5. Section F says that employers should take all necessary steps to prevent sexual harassment from occurring in the first place. This includes policy statements, training for employees, and grievance procedures.

6. Section G says that if one employee submits to sexual requests and gains benefits thereby, other employees, equally well qualified, may sue on the basis of sex discrimination for not being allowed those same benefits or opportunities. If a supervisor gives the best job assignments to a subordinate because of their sexual activities, other employees, both male and female, could claim sex discrimination because they were denied those job assignments. This section of the Guidelines was upheld by a federal court in Delaware.

But the question, what does the law say, is just like the other questions—it has no simple answer either. What "the law" says can be interpreted to mean what the EEOC Guidelines say, what the 1964 Civil Rights Act says, what the courts are saying, or a combination of all three. A good basic answer is to think in these terms—for behavior to be considered illegal sexual harassment, it must meet these criteria:

• It occurs because of the person's sex—it is related to or about sex.

• It is unwelcome, not returned, not mutual.

• It affects the terms or conditions of employment, including the work environment itself.

Broad Legal Definitions Help Women Fight Harassment

by Susan Gluck Mezey

About the author: *Susan Gluck Mezey is a professor of political science and women's studies at Loyola University in Chicago.*

Despite the widespread occurrences of sexual harassment in the workplace, for a long time it was a problem with no name—each victim struggling with it on an individual basis. Women were reluctant to report episodes of harassment; they felt shamed, embarrassed, and fearful of losing their jobs if they brought attention to it. When women began to take their cases to the federal courts, the majority of courts dismissed their suits without even examining the evidence. Federal court judges ruled that even if plaintiffs were telling the truth about what happened to them at work, their employers' and supervisors' actions did not violate the law.

In her path-breaking work on sexual harassment in the workplace, Catharine MacKinnon distinguishes between two types of behavior: *quid pro quo* harassment and condition of work harassment. The harassment labeled *quid pro quo* occurs when a person in authority, typically a male, requires sexual favors from an employee, typically a female, in return for an employment advantage. Advantages include getting hired, getting promoted, obtaining better working conditions, and not getting fired.

Work Harassment

Condition of work harassment, also known as environmental or workplace harassment, is less direct and arises when an employee, again typically a female, is subjected to requests for sexual favors, sexual comments, or sexual insults but no negative employment consequences follow from the employee's refusal to accede to the demands made on her. MacKinnon asserts that

> unwanted sexual advances, made simply because she has a woman's body, can
> be a daily part of a woman's work life. She may be constantly felt or pinched,
> visually undressed and stared at, surreptitiously kissed, commented upon, ma-
> nipulated into being found alone, and generally taken advantage of at work—
> but never promised or denied anything explicitly connected with her job. . . .

In *Williams v. Saxbe*, a 1976 decision, the first sexual harassment suit succeeded in federal district court. Diane Williams, an information officer for the
Department of Justice, brought suit
when she was fired from her job less
than two weeks after she refused her
supervisor's sexual advances. For
the first time, a court recognized a
link between a supervisor's conduct
and a victim's employment status
and agreed that a plaintiff had made
a legitimate claim of sex discrimination. Rejecting the argument that sexual demands could be made to both sexes, the district court found that the actions of
her supervisors "created an artificial barrier to employment which was placed
before one gender and not the other."

> *"Despite the widespread*
> *occurrences of sexual*
> *harassment in the workplace,*
> *for a long time it was a*
> *problem with no name."*

The EEOC Guidelines

At the same time that the courts became more accepting of sexual harassment
suits, the Equal Employment Opportunity Commission issued guidelines reaf-
firming the linkage between sexual harassment and employment discrimination. Based in large part on prevailing Title VII case law, the guidelines were
formally added as an amendment to the EEOC Guidelines on Discrimination
Based on Sex.

On April 11, 1980, the EEOC published a set of interim guidelines on sexual
harassment and, after a public comment period of sixty days, drafted the final
regulations. They were then released on November 10, 1980. Going beyond
case law, the guidelines accomplished the two major tasks of providing a com-
prehensive definition of sexual harassment, including both *quid pro quo* and
workplace harassment, and expanding the prevailing view on employer liability.

The 1980 guidelines stated that

> (a) Unwelcome sexual advances, requests for sexual favors, and other verbal
> or physical conduct of a sexual nature constitute sexual harassment when (1)
> submission to such conduct is made either explicitly or implicitly a term or
> condition of an individual's employment, (2) submission to or rejection of
> such conduct by an individual is used as a basis for employment decisions af-
> fecting such individual, or (3) such conduct has the purpose or effect of unrea-
> sonably interfering with an individual's work performance or creating an in-
> timidating, hostile, or offensive working environment.

The EEOC's position on a company's liability for harassment by supervisory personnel was a broad one. The commission urged that the company be held strictly liable even if the harassment violated company policy and was unknown to company officials. The guidelines made no distinctions between hostile environment harassment and *quid pro quo* harassment when supervisors were involved. When other employees (nonsupervisors) were the harassers, the guidelines placed responsibility on the company if officials knew or should have known about the harassment and failed to take corrective measures.

Hostile Environment Harassment

The judiciary proved to be more sympathetic to *quid pro quo* harassment suits than to hostile environment suits because it was more apparent in *quid pro quo* cases that the harassment affected the employee's terms and conditions of employment. Because the courts were not convinced that workplace harassment violated Title VII, these cases were less successful in court. Then, in 1981, in *Bundy v. Jackson*, the District of Columbia Circuit recognized that a woman could be injured when sexual harassment created a hostile work environment.

The district court had ruled that Title VII did not forbid the harassment experienced by Sandra Bundy, an officer with the Department of Corrections. The judge dismissed her complaint on the grounds that she was not denied employment benefits—that is, she was not fired for refusing her superiors' sexual advances. He found

> *"The commission urged that the company be held strictly liable even if the harassment violated company policy and was unknown to company officials."*

that "the making of improper sexual advances to female employees [was] standard operating procedure, a fact of life, a normal condition of employment in the office."

The court's finding was substantiated by the tales of the sexual propositions directed at Bundy, including the one by a high-level supervisor who, when she complained to him of his subordinates' actions, told her that "any man in his right mind would want to rape you." Despite these incidents, the district court denied Sandra Bundy relief because it found that sexual attention toward female employees was only sport for her supervisors and a "game" played without retaliation for refusing to play.

On appeal, the circuit court recognized that Bundy was a victim of sex discrimination within the bounds of Title VII. The court cited "numerous cases finding Title VII violations where an employer created or condoned a substantially discriminatory work *environment*, regardless of whether the complaining employees lost any tangible job benefits as a result of the discrimination." Ruling otherwise, said the court, would subject a woman to a "cruel trilemma" [in which] she can endure the harassment. [Or] she can attempt to oppose it, with little hope of success, either legal or practical, but with every prospect of making the job even less tolerable for her. Or she can leave her job, with little hope of legal relief and the likely prospect of another job where she will face harassment anew.

The sexual harassment case that eventually reached the Supreme Court began a few years after *Bundy* was decided, when Mechelle Vinson filed suit against her supervisor, Sidney Taylor, and her employer, the Capital City Federal Savings and Loan Association. Vinson had been hired initially as a teller-trainee and was subsequently promoted to teller, head teller, and then assistant branch manager. After working at the branch for four years, she took indefinite sick leave and was fired for excessive time on leave.

> *"Under the guidelines, an employer is accountable for sexual harassment committed by its supervisory personnel."*

The Vinson Case

At a trial that lasted eleven days, Vinson testified that Taylor propositioned her and, after initially refusing him, that she ultimately capitulated because she was afraid of losing her job. She claimed that she was forced to submit to him during the day as well as after work, that he touched her in front of other employees, that he followed her into the women's room where he exposed himself to her, and that he assaulted and even raped her. She testified that she had sexual intercourse with him forty or fifty times during the three-year period that the harassment continued. She did not report him, she said, because she was afraid.

Taylor completely denied her story, and the savings and loan disassociated itself from him, saying that if he committed these acts, he did so without its knowledge or authorization. Following the trial, the district court judge ruled that Vinson had failed to make out a Title VII claim of sex discrimination. Even though this disposed of the case, the lower court did not stop there but went on to assess the savings and loan's liability as well. Because it had a policy against discrimination, and because Vinson had never complained about Taylor, the court concluded that the savings and loan could not be held accountable for Taylor's actions, if indeed, he committed the acts of which he was accused.

The District of Columbia Circuit Court reversed on appeal. . . . Referring to the EEOC guidelines, the court held that Title VII applied to both [environmental and *quid pro quo*] harassment. It remanded the case to the district court for a determination on whether Taylor's actions created a hostile environment.

In remanding, the circuit court also instructed the district court on how to decide several points of law. The district court did not determine whether Vinson and Taylor actually had a sexual relationship; it merely ruled that if they did, it was voluntary and irrelevant to her employment status. In reaching its finding of voluntariness, the lower court had allowed Taylor to introduce evidence relating to Vinson's dress and sexual fantasies.

Involuntary Acquiescence

The appellate court rejected the view that Vinson's "voluntary" acquiescence to Taylor's sexual demands, that is, that she was not forced into having sex with him against her will, defeated her claim. Quoting the EEOC definition of sexual harassment as "unwelcome sexual advances . . . [that have] the purpose or effect of unreasonably interfering with an individual's work performance or creating an intimidating, hostile or offensive working environment," the appellate court stressed that her "voluntariness" was immaterial. Because Congress did not intend a victim to forfeit her right to complain when she was forced to capitulate to sexual demands to keep her job, evidence of Vinson's clothing and sexual fantasies were irrelevant.

The district court had not permitted Vinson to present evidence that Taylor had sexually harassed other female employees, and here too, the appellate court disagreed. The circuit court felt it was relevant to her case that Taylor created a sexually harassing environment for female employees.

Finally, and perhaps most important, the appellate court rejected the lower court view of the employer's responsibility. The grievance procedure required an employee to file a complaint with the supervisor; in this case, because Taylor was the supervisor, Vinson could not comply with the rules. She contended that her employer had notice of Taylor's harassment by other means. The lower court disagreed and refused to hold the savings and loan liable, reasoning that even if Taylor were guilty of sexual harassment, the employer was unaware of it. . . . In *Vinson*, the district court absolved the employer from responsibility, believing the claim that it was unaware of Taylor's harassment of women employees under his supervision.

> *"The Court ruled that trial courts must examine the facts of each case to determine when employers are to be held responsible for their supervisors' acts."*

The circuit court pointed out that Title VII forbids discrimination by employers *and* by their agents. And the court held that as an "agent" of the savings and loan, Taylor's violation of Title VII was attributable to his employer, regardless of its knowledge of his behavior. Justifying its decision to assess far-reaching employer liability for the acts of its employees (known as vicarious liability), the circuit court pointed to legislative debate on Title VII. Although there was no evidence that Congress intended to impose vicarious liability, the court believed it significant that Congress had at least discussed the issue and had not ruled it out.

Finding the EEOC guidelines "persuasive," the circuit court accepted the broad interpretation of employer liability. Under the guidelines, an employer is accountable for sexual harassment committed by its supervisory personnel "regardless of whether the specific acts complained of were authorized or even forbidden by the employer and regardless of whether the employer knew or should have known of their occurrence." Moreover, added the court, Title VII case law generally considers supervisory personnel as agents of their employers and holds employers accountable for their acts.

The court broadly defined an agent not only as a supervisory employee, but as any employee with authority to hire and fire. An employee who has power over a subordinate can threaten and coerce and, thereby, harass. While Taylor could not hire or fire, he had authority to recommend salary levels and promotions. The court wanted to create a disincentive for the employer to look the other way and escape responsibility simply by disclaiming knowledge of the harassment. "Much of the promise of Title VII will become empty," declared the court, "if victims of unlawful discrimination cannot secure redress from the only source capable of providing it."

> *"The Supreme Court acknowledged that sexual harassment was an unfair condition of work— based on sex."*

The Supreme Court Rules on Sexual Harassment

Vinson's employer, now known as the Meritor Savings Bank, appealed to the Supreme Court. In 1986, a unanimous Court, with Justice William Rehnquist announcing the opinion, affirmed the circuit court's ruling to send the case back to the district court for a trial on Vinson's complaint of hostile environment harassment. The Supreme Court, however, rejected the circuit court's expansive interpretation of vicarious liability as well as its ruling that evidence of the employee's provocation was inadmissible. Despite these reservations, the high court affirmed the circuit court's holding that a hostile work environment created by sexual harassment violates Title VII even in the absence of demands for sexual favors or loss of tangible job benefits.

The bank argued that legislative history and settled case law show that Title VII protection is limited to sexual discrimination that erects "tangible, economic barriers." Not true, said Rehnquist. The injury caused by the discrimination need not be economic. Title VII was intended to reach an entire array of employment disparity between the sexes. Rehnquist also pointed out that the EEOC guidelines clearly state that Title VII extends to complaints of a hostile environment. Cautioning that not all incidents of offensive or annoying behavior in the workplace would amount to harassment, he agreed that the conduct described by Vinson was sufficiently "severe" and "pervasive" to constitute harassment. On these grounds, the Court affirmed the circuit court's decision to remand.

Rehnquist cited a number of errors the appellate court had made in interpreting sexual harassment law. He found that the appellate court had correctly ruled that it was irrelevant whether Vinson was a voluntary participant in the sexual relationship. The key question, Rehnquist said, was not whether she voluntarily engaged in sex with him but whether the sexual advances were "unwelcome." And although the circuit court had flatly stated that Vinson's dress or speech "had no place in this litigation," the Supreme Court disagreed and held these were relevant in determining whether the sexual attention was welcome to her.

Straddling the Fence

The Court straddled the fence on the issue of the employer's vicarious liability for hostile environment harassment. On the one hand, it refused to impose strict liability in workplace harassment cases. On the other hand, it held that a company would not be relieved of responsibility merely by claiming that it lacked notice of the supervisor's actions. Nor would it be absolved by simply pointing to the existence of a nondiscrimination policy or showing that the victim did not use a company grievance procedure.

The Supreme Court was unwilling to commit to a clear statement on employers' liability in part because of the EEOC's apparent shift in direction. Notwithstanding its earlier guidelines creating strict employer liability whenever supervisory personnel were involved, the EEOC now argued in its brief to the Court, filed by the solicitor general, that while strict company liability for the acts of agents is appropriate in a *quid pro quo* case, it is not suitable for a workplace harassment suit. In a hostile environment case, the EEOC now urged, employer liability should rest on two factors: whether the employer had an express policy against harassment and a grievance procedure to resolve complaints; and whether the employer knew of the harassment and failed to take action to remedy it.

The Supreme Court adopted a middle ground between the circuit court and the EEOC. It refused to impose automatic liability for sexual harassment by supervisors on the employer, agreeing with the revised EEOC position that employers must have notice in order to be held liable in a hostile environment case. But because Congress intended that Title VII be interpreted as holding employers accountable for *some* of the acts of their employees, the Court held that mere "absence of notice to an employer does not necessarily insulate that employer from liability." Advocating a case-by-case approach, the

> *"Sexual harassment is inextricably intertwined with the status of women in the workforce."*

Court ruled that trial courts must examine the facts of each case to determine when employers are to be held responsible for their supervisors' acts.

Finally, the Court criticized the bank's grievance policy because it was a general policy against discrimination that did not specifically forbid harassment. It required the employee to direct complaints to her supervisor, a questionable procedure when, as here, the supervisor is the harasser. Thus, after more than a decade of litigation, the Supreme Court acknowledged that sexual harassment was an unfair condition of work—based on sex—and could be addressed in a Title VII lawsuit. In *Vinson*, the Court went even further to allow suits for harassment that polluted the work environment, even in the absence of material losses in the woman's employment status.

Shortcomings of the *Vinson* Decision

While *Vinson* advanced sexual equality in the workplace, the decision had two major shortcomings. First, the Supreme Court permitted evidence of the employee's dress, manner, and speech to be introduced at trial as a defense to the harassment charge. Evidence such as this allows supervisors to claim that the employees "asked for" the harassment or that they "enjoyed" it. Second, *Vinson* took a step back from the more stringent—original—EEOC position on the issue of employer liability for workplace harassment.

Some justices objected to the Court's retrenchment on employer liability. Thurgood Marshall, speaking for himself and William Brennan, Harry Blackmun, and John Paul Stevens, concurred in the Court's judgment to affirm the appellate court's decision, but wrote separately to express disapproval of the high court's ruling on employer liability for environmental harassment. Marshall pointed out that under Title VII law, expressed in the 1980 EEOC guidelines, the employer is always liable for harassment by supervisory employees—whether *quid pro quo* or workplace harassment. Lack of notice to the employer is not a defense. He saw no "justification for a special rule, to be applied *only* in 'hostile environment' cases, that sexual harassment does not create employer liability until the employee suffering the discrimination notifies other supervisors."

Sexual harassment is inextricably intertwined with the status of women in the workforce. "Whether at the office or the factory, sexual harassment is nothing more than the assertion of power by men over women, perceived to be in a vulnerable position with respect to male authority."

In her study of sexual harassment, MacKinnon argued that sexual harassment stems from an abuse of power rather than sexual desire; she attributed the problem to women's subordinate position in the labor force. Women are victimized by harassment because they "are generally men's subordinates on the job, with men in the position to do the hiring, firing, supervising, and promoting."

Legal Definitions of Sexual Harassment Must Be Broad

by Deborah L. Siegel

About the author: *Deborah L. Siegel compiled and wrote the report* Sexual Harassment: Research and Resources *for the National Council for Research on Women (NCRW). NCRW is a coalition of centers and organizations that conducts feminist research, policy analysis, and educational programs.*

The assumption that sexual harassment of women is harmless, trivial, or easy for women to handle is wrong. What one researcher calls "women's hidden occupational hazard," sexual harassment is sexual victimization. It is not a benign mating ritual but an invidious form of sex discrimination. The clear consensus among researchers is that sexual harassment, which affects an estimated one out of every two women, is an issue of power, not sex. To be adjudicated fairly, sexual harassment must be understood as part of the continuum of violence against women.

The Accuser Becomes the Accused

In a typical sexual harassment case, the female accuser becomes the accused and the victim is twice victimized. Threatened by the charge, a male harasser frequently will go to great lengths to discredit his accuser. Underlying the dynamics of the situation is profound distrust of a woman's word and a serious power differential between the accuser and the accused. Barbara Gutek, a professor in the Department of Management and Policy at the University of Arizona, Tucson, notes that "for a woman to say that she has been harassed is not enough for people to believe her." Popular myth—and some members of the Senate Judiciary Committee—would have us believe that a woman who is "*really* sexually harassed" immediately reports the incident, cuts off all connections with her harasser, and goes on with her life and career. Contrary to such assumptions, studies show that for a victim of sexual harassment, timely, peremptory response is the exception, not the norm.

It is economically impossible for many victims to sever ties with their harassers, who are often also their superiors, and many women fear that complaining about co-workers will brand them as trouble-makers. Women currently make up nearly half of the paid work-force. By the year 2000, nearly two-thirds of all new entrants into the work-force will

> *"To be adjudicated fairly, sexual harassment must be understood as part of the continuum of violence against women."*

be women. Surveys suggest that the rate of sexual harassment has remained relatively stable over the years. Yet in the years between 1984 and 1988, the number of sexual harassment complaints filed with the Equal Employment Opportunity Commission (EEOC) dipped twice—from 4,953 in 1985 to 4,431 in 1986 and from 5,336 in 1987 to 5,215 in 1988. Only 5,557 complaints were filed in 1990. Research on sexual harassment offers multiple reasons for the lack of formal complaints, among them the fact that legal mechanisms for processing complaints are ineffective while at the same time emotional and financial costs to the victim are often devastating.

The need to help victims of sexual harassment break their silence has never been more compelling. The need is especially pressing for female victims. Males do experience sexual harassment, but studies show that women are nine times more likely than men to quit a job because of sexual harassment, five times more likely to transfer, and three times more likely to lose a job. Says Stephanie Edelstein, Sexual Harassment Educational Director at the University of California, Davis, "We must seek solutions within institutions that allow for a safe place for women to come forward. We must learn how to handle cases so that neither person becomes destroyed, and we must work to change the culture of the places in which we work.". . .

What Is Sexual Harassment?

Until recently, few people openly discussed sexual harassment. And as Louise Fitzgerald, a psychologist at the University of Illinois at Champaign-Urbana points out, we still lack a common definition. The first federal statute prohibiting sex discrimination in the workplace was not passed until the 1960s; the phrase *sexual harassment* was not coined until the mid-1970s; and the U.S. Supreme Court did not recognize sexual harassment until 1986.

"It is not surprising . . . that women would not complain of an experience for which there has been no name. Until 1976, lacking a term to express it, sexual harassment was literally unspeakable, which made generalized, shared and social definitions of it inaccessible," [states Catharine MacKinnon].

144

Sexual Harassment

Originally thought to be limited to those relatively rare situations where women are compelled to trade sexual favors for professional survival (known as *quid pro quo*), sexual harassment is now recognized more broadly as "the inappropriate sexualization of an otherwise nonsexual relationship, an assertion by men of the primacy of a woman's sexuality over her role as worker, [professional colleague,] or student," [according to Louise F. Fitzgerald and A.J. Ormerod].

Legal scholars like Catharine MacKinnon, a professor at the School of Law, University of Michigan, and activists like Susan Brownmiller are credited with initiating the view of sexual harassment that has radically changed the way sexual harassment complaints are treated under the legal system. Shifting the focus of sexual harassment from the belief that males' sexual pursuit of women in the workplace or the classroom is essentially biological and that sexual harassment is therefore a "normal" consequence of attraction between the sexes, MacKinnon, Brownmiller, and others advocate a "dominance" approach. In *The Sexual Harassment of Working Women*, MacKinnon claims that "sexual harassment, most broadly defined, refers to the unwanted imposition of sexual requirements in the context of a relationship of unequal power." Based on her analysis of legal cases and her examination of sexual harassment as women report experiencing it, MacKinnon explains why sexual harassment *is* sex discrimination. It occurs in the workplace because women occupy largely inferior job positions and roles. At the same time it also works to keep women "in their place."

Legal Definitions

"The law sees and treats women the way men see and treat women," [states Catharine MacKinnon].

The first litigation of sexual harassment claims did not occur until the mid-seventies. Title VII of the 1964 Civil Rights Act prohibiting sex discrimination in the workplace was followed eight years later by Title IX of the 1972 Higher Education Amendments prohibiting sex discrimination in educational institutions receiving federal assistance. But in much of the early adjudication of sex discrimination, the phenomenon of sexual harassment was typically seen "as isolated and idiosyncratic, or as natural and universal, and, in either case, as inappropriate for legal intervention," [according to Deborah Rhode]. It was not until 1980 that the Equal Employment Opportunity Commission, in its "Guidelines on Discrimination," explicitly defined sexual harassment under Title VII as a form of unlawful, sex-based discrimination. In 1984, the guidelines were expanded to include educational institutions. Accord-

> *"Sexual harassment is now recognized more broadly as 'the inappropriate sexualization of an otherwise nonsexual relationship.'"*

145

ing to the 1984 EEOC "Policy Statement on Sexual Harassment,"

Unwelcome sexual advances, requests for sexual favors, and other verbal or physical conduct of a sexual nature constitutes sexual harassment when

(1) submission to such conduct is made either explicitly or implicitly a term or condition of an individual's employment or academic advancement,

(2) submission to or rejection of such conduct by an individual is used as the basis for employment decisions or academic decisions affecting such individual, or

(3) such conduct has the purpose or effect of unreasonably interfering with an individual's work or academic performance or creating an intimidating, hostile, or offensive working or academic environment.

In 1986, the Supreme Court, in a unanimous decision in *Meritor Savings Bank, FSB v. Vinson*, upheld this interpretation of Title VII and the EEOC guidelines that define as prohibited discrimination the existence of a hostile or threatening work environment. Rejecting the contention that Title VII prohibits only discrimination that causes tangible economic harm, the Court ruled instead that under Title VII employees have the right to work in environments free from discriminatory intimidation, ridicule, and insult.

Quid Pro Quo Harassment

The law does make a distinction between *quid pro quo* cases that fall under Section (2) of the EEOC guidelines, in which the harassment involves trading sex for work, and cases that fall under Section (3), "hostile environment" or what MacKinnon calls "conditions of work harassment," in which unwanted and offensive sexual behavior is present in the workplace but not attached to job-related financial detriment or reward.

While the language and terms of Sections (1) and (2) of the EEOC guidelines are clear, the language in Section (3) defining a "hostile environment" has allowed considerable latitude for interpretation, continuing to cause confusion and ambiguity both in and out of the courts. Comments such as, "Can't you take a joke?" "You're being overly sensitive," and "Lighten up!" are painfully familiar to any

> *"Sexual harassment, most broadly defined, refers to the unwanted imposition of sexual requirements in the context of a relationship of unequal power."*

woman who has experienced the humiliation of sexual harassment. In all cases, the burden of proof for sexual harassment and "hostile environment" falls entirely on the accuser. Says Stephanie Riger, Professor of Sociology at the University of Illinois, Champaign-Urbana, "Courts have required that incidents falling into [Section (3)] . . . be repeated in order to establish that such an envi-

146

ronment exists; these incidents must be both pervasive and so severe that they affect the victim's psychological well-being."

Victims' rights to collect damages continue to be limited under federal law. While the 1991 Civil Rights Act, which recently passed the Senate, does not limit awards for back pay and past out-of-pocket damages like medical bills, the compromise forged to ensure passage of the bill in Congress and gain White House approval limits other damages according to the size of the employer's work-force. Unlike the potential damages available to victims of racial discrimination, damages for sex discrimination are capped at $50,000 for small companies and $300,000 for larger ones.

The "Reasonable Person" Rule

As the law has been interpreted, prohibition against sexual harassment in the workplace technically covers any remark or behavior that is sufficiently severe and pervasive that not only the victim's but also a "reasonable person's" psychological well-being would be affected. But a 1991 landmark ruling by the Court of Appeals for the Ninth Circuit in California held that "the appropriate perspective for judging a hostile environment claim is that of the 'reasonable woman'" and recognized that a woman's perspective may differ substantially from a man's. In his ruling, Judge Robert Beezer observed, "Conduct that many men consider unobjectionable may offend many women." Because women are much

> *"The appropriate perspective for judging a hostile environment claim is that of the 'reasonable woman.'"*

more likely to be victims of rape and sexual assault, women have a "stronger incentive to be concerned with sexual behavior." Michele Paludi, Professor of Psychology at Hunter College, City University of New York, points out there may also be "a difference between intent and impact. Many [men] may not intend it, but some things they do may be experienced by women as sexual harassment. A touch or comment can be seen very differently."

While the 1991 Ninth Circuit Court ruling acknowledges that men and women may interpret the same behavior differently, in application this legal understanding is often overshadowed by a grave misunderstanding of the nature of sexual harassment as experienced by its victims. Says Susan Estrich, Professor of Law at University of Southern California, "The people doing the judging are in no position to understand the position of those being judged. The powerful make judgments against the powerless."

Stephanie Riger notes that "the dilemma in applying [the 'reasonable person' standard] to sexual harassment is that a reasonable woman and a reasonable man are likely to differ in their judgment of what is offensive." And Riger adds, "Men's judgments about what behavior constitutes harassment, and who is to blame, are likely to prevail." Deborah Rhode, Professor of Law at Stanford Law School, points out that in terms of the court, what constitutes harassment—and what determines the amounts of awards for damages under state law and in the future under federal law—"ultimately depends on the perceptions of the judge rather than the victim, and the vestiges of long-standing prejudices do not seem entirely absent from judicial as well as workplace forums."

Research-Based Definitions

As a result of such legal gray areas, researchers have constructed more explicit definitions based on sexual harassment as women report experiencing it. Sexually harassing behavior falls into categories, differing in severity. Such definitions aim for clearer understanding of what constitutes a "hostile environment." One of the most widely used models breaks harassing behavior into five basic types of sexual harassment:

Five Types of Sexual Harassment

Type 1: Gender Harassment
    generalized sexist remarks and behavior

Type 2: Seductive Behavior
    inappropriate and offensive, but essentially sanction-free behavior, with no penalty attached to noncompliance

Type 3: Sexual Bribery
    solicitation of sexual activity or other sex-linked behavior by promise of rewards

Type 4: Sexual Coercion
    coercion of sexual activity by threat of punishment

Type 5: Sexual Imposition or Assault
    gross sexual imposition like touching, fondling, grabbing, or assault

Researchers agree that women link different kinds of sexualized behavior in the workplace in ways that men, on the average, do not. Says Mary Rowe, Special Assistant to the President at Massachusetts Institute of Technology, "Mild sexualized behavior such as flirting or joking is often seen as sexualized by the woman and not by the man."

Research literature documenting perceptions of sexual harassment—by whom and when a particular behavior will be interpreted as sexual harassment—is fairly well developed. Variables analyzed include the gender

"Sexually harassing behavior falls into categories, differing in severity."

of the perceiver, severity and explicitness of the behavior, status of the initiator, degree of power in the relationship between the individuals involved, behavior of the victim, and attitudes of the perceiver (most notably attitudes about feminism). In all the studies, gender has clearly proven to be the most influential factor in determining whether incidents will be defined as sexual harassment, with women universally more likely to label a given situation as harassing than men.

When college men and women were presented with hypothetical scenarios, for example, women spotted harassment at much earlier stages. In one scenario, a male department chair invites a new female employee to lunch to discuss her work. He focuses the lunchtime conversation on her personal life. On another occasion, over drinks, he tries to fondle her. "Most

> *"Gender has clearly proven to be the most influential factor in determining whether incidents will be defined as sexual harassment."*

of the women said that sexual harassment started at the first lunch, when he talked about her private life instead of her work. Most of the men said that sexual harassment began at the point he fondled her," [states Michele Paludi].

In a study conducted by Barbara Gutek, 67% of men surveyed said they would be complimented if they were propositioned by a woman at work. Only 17% of women said they would take such a proposition as a compliment.

Women's Definitions

Most women who are sexually harassed never say anything. In the 1987 U.S. Merit Systems Protection Board survey of federal employees, only 5% of those who indicated they had experienced sexual harassment actually filed formal complaints or requested investigations. Experts on the issue agree that the overwhelming majority of sexual harassment goes unreported. [Freada Klein states that] "In most organizations, at least 90% of sexual harassment victims are unwilling to come forward for two reasons: fear of retaliation and fear of loss of privacy."

Regardless of whether they formally voice a complaint, when *do* women say it is a problem? According to Claire Safran, in her survey for *Redbook Magazine* in 1976, "Objection to sexual harassment at work is not a neopuritan moral protest against signs of attraction, displays of affection, compliments, flirtation, or touching on the job. Instead, women are rattled and often angry about sex that is one-sided, unwelcome, or comes with strings attached. When it's something a woman wants to turn off but can't (a co-worker or supervisor who refuses to stop) or when it's coming from someone with the economic power to hire or fire, help or hinder, reward or punish (an employer or client who mustn't be offended)—that's when [women] say it's a problem."

The resignation of one of the nation's first female neurosurgeons from her senior faculty position at Stanford Medical School dramatized one woman's saying "it's a problem." Dr. Frances Conley reported that her male colleagues called her "honey" in the operating room and fondled her legs under the table.

Stanford medical students also reported that slides of *Playboy* centerfolds were still being used to "spice up" lectures. Although Dr. Conley has since resumed her position, when asked what finally made her quit, she noted that the problems had not lessened in more than 20 years and a colleague who was seen as responsible for harassing was promoted to a senior administrative post at the medical school. "I had not realized how pervasive the sexism was," Conley responded. "I couldn't brush it off. I couldn't pretend to be one of the boys any longer."

The Continuum of Violence

"Sexual harassment . . . is the most recent form of victimization of women to be redefined as a social rather than a personal problem, following rape and wife abuse," [states Stephanie Riger].

Susan Estrich examines similarities between the doctrines of rape law and the legal tools used in sexual harassment cases: "The rules and prejudices have been borrowed almost wholesale from traditional rape law. The focus on the conduct of the woman—her reactions or lack of them, her resistance or lack of it— reappears with only the most minor changes." Estrich's analysis of the rulings that have shaped sexual harassment law illuminates the durability of sexism in the law's judgment of the sexual relations of men and women.

Like rape, sexual harassment is not an issue of lust; it is an issue of power. Sexual harassment *must* be seen as part of a continuum of sexual victimization that ranges from staring and leering to assault and rape. "Most sexual harassment starts at the subtle end of the continuum and escalates over time. Each year, 1% of women in the U.S. labor force are sexually assaulted on the job," [according to Freada Klein]. Yet cultural mythologies consistently blame the victim for sexual abuse and act to keep women "in their place." Scholars have identified several similarities in attitudes toward rape and sexual harassment, essentially revealing cultural myths that blame the victim:

> *"Sexual harassment . . . is the most recent form of victimization of women to be redefined as a social rather than a personal problem."*

1. *Women ask for it*
Rape: Victims "seduce" their rapists.
Sexual Harassment: Sexual harassment is a form of seduction; women precipitate harassment by the way they dress and talk.

2. *Women say no but mean yes*
Rape: Women secretly need and want to be forced into sex. They don't know what they want.

Sexual Harassment: Women like the attention. Harassment usually continues or escalates when the victim has given no positive response or a negative response. Harassers offer such excuses as "I know her better than she knows herself."

3. *Women lie*

Rape: In most charges of "rape," the woman is lying.

Sexual Harassment: Women lie about sexual harassment in order to get men they dislike in trouble.

Perhaps the most dangerous of these myths is the assumption that since women seem to "go along" with sexual harassment, they must like it, which means that sexual harassment is not really harassment at all. But as researcher Lynn Wehrli points out, "This constitutes more than a simplistic denial of all we know about the ways in which socialization and economic dependence foster submissiveness and override free choice. . . . Those women who are able to speak out about sexual harassment use terms such as *humiliating, intimidating, frightening, financially damaging, embarrassing, nerve-wracking, awful,* and *frustrating.* . . . These are hardly words used to describe a situation which one 'likes.' "

The "Reasonable Woman" Is an Effective Standard to Establish Harassment

by Ellen Goodman

About the author: *Ellen Goodman is a nationally syndicated columnist.*

Since the volatile mix of sex and harassment exploded under the Capitol dome, it hasn't just been senators scurrying for cover. The case of the professor and judge has left a gender gap that looks more like a crater.

We have discovered that men and women see this issue differently. Stop the presses. Sweetheart, get me rewrite.

On the "Today" show, Bryant Gumbel asks something about a man's right to have a pinup on the wall and Katie Couric says what she thinks of that. On the normally sober "MacNeil/Lehrer" hour the usual panel of legal experts doesn't break down between left and right but between male and female.

Shared Experiences

On a hundred radio talk shows, women are sharing experiences and men are asking for proof. In ten thousand offices, the order of the day is the nervous joke. One boss asks his secretary if he can still say "good morning," or is that sexual harassment. Heh, heh. The women aren't laughing.

Okay boys and girls, back to your corners. Can we talk? Can we hear?

The good news is that women have stopped rolling their eyes at each other and started speaking out. The bad news is that we may each assume the other gender not only doesn't understand but can't understand. "They don't get it" becomes "they can't get it."

Let's start with the fact that sexual harassment is a concept as new as date rape. Date rape, that should-be oxymoron, assumes a different perspective on the part of the man and the woman. His date, her rape. Sexual harassment

Ellen Goodman, "The Reasonable Woman Standard," *Liberal Opinion*, October 21, 1991, © 1991, The Boston Globe Newspaper Co./Washington Post Writers Group. Reprinted with permission.

comes with some of the same assumptions. What he labels sexual, she labels harassment.

This produces what many men tend to darkly call a "murky" area of the law. Murky however is a step in the right direction. When everything was clear, it was clearly biased. The old single standard was male standard. The only options a working woman had were to grin, bear it or quit.

Women's Feelings

Sexual harassment rules are based on the point of view of the victim, nearly always a woman. The rules ask, not just whether she has been physically assaulted, but whether the environment in which she works is intimidating or coercive. Whether she feels harassed. It says that her feelings matter.

This of course, raises all sorts of hackles about women's *feelings*, women's *sensitivity*. How can you judge the sensitivity level of every single woman you work with? What's a poor man to do?

But the law isn't psychiatry. It doesn't adapt to individual sensitivity levels. There is a standard emerging by which the courts can judge these cases and by which people can judge them as well. It's called "the reasonable woman standard." How would a reasonable woman interpret this? How would a reasonable woman behave?

This is not an entirely new idea, although perhaps the law's belief in the reasonableness of women is. There has long been a "reasonable man" in the law not to mention a "reasonable pilot," a "reasonable innkeeper," a "reasonable train operator."

> *"Sexual harassment is a concept as new as date rape."*

Now the law is admitting that a reasonable woman may see these situations differently than a man. That truth—available in your senator's mailbag—is also apparent in research. We tend to see sexualized situations from our own gender's perspective. Kim Lane Scheppele, a political science and law professor at the University of Michigan, summarizes the miscues this way: "Men see the sex first and miss the coercion. Women see the coercion and miss the sex."

Another Perspective

Does that mean that we are genetically doomed to our double vision? Scheppele is quick to say no. Our justice system rests on the belief that one person can get in another's head, walk in her shoes, see things from another perspective. And so does our hope for change.

If a jury of car drivers can understand how a "reasonable pilot" would see one situation, a jury of men can see how a reasonable woman would see another event. The crucial ingredient is empathy.

Check it out in the office tomorrow. He's coming on, she's backing off, he keeps coming. Read the body language. There's a playboy calendar on the wall and a PMS joke in the boardroom and the boss is just being friendly. How would a reasonable woman feel?

At this moment, when the air is crackling with hostility and consciousness-raising has the hair sticking up on the back of many necks, guess what? Men can "get it." Reasonable men.

Feminist Legal Definitions of Sexual Harassment Can Be Effectively Used in the Courts

by Catharine A. MacKinnon

About the author: *Catharine A. MacKinnon is a professor at the University of Michigan's law school. She represented Mechelle Vinson as co-counsel in the Supreme Court case of 1986 that now provides the legal definition of sexual harassment.*

Sexual harassment, the event, is not new to women. It is the law of injuries that it is new to. Sexual pressure imposed on someone who is not in an economic position to refuse it became sex discrimination in the midseventies, and in education soon afterward. It became possible to do something legal about sexual harassment because some women took women's experience of violation seriously enough to design a law around it, as if what happens to women matters. This was apparently such a startling way of proceeding that sexual harassment was protested as a feminist invention. Sexual harassment, the event, was not invented by feminists; the perpetrators did that with no help from us. Sexual harassment, the legal claim—the idea that the law should see it the way its victims see it—is definitely a feminist invention. Feminists first took women's experience seriously enough to uncover this problem and conceptualize it and pursue it legally. That legal claim is just beginning to produce more than a handful of reported cases. Ten years later, "[i]t may well be that sex harassment is the hottest present day Title VII issue." It is time for a down-the-road assessment of this departure.

The law against sexual harassment is a practical attempt to stop a form of exploitation. It is also one test of sexual politics as feminist jurisprudence, of possibilities for social change for women through law. The existence of a law against sexual harassment has affected both the context of meaning within which social life is lived and the concrete delivery of rights through the legal system. The sexually harassed have been given a name for their suffering and an analysis that connects it with gender. They have been given a forum, legitimacy to speak, authority to make claims, and an avenue for possible relief. Before, what happened to them was all right. Now it is not.

> *"The law against sexual harassment is a practical attempt to stop a form of exploitation."*

This matters. Sexual abuse mutes victims socially through the violation itself. Often the abuser enforces secrecy and silence; secrecy and silence may be part of what is so sexy about sexual abuse. When the state also forecloses a validated space for denouncing and rectifying the victimization, it seals this secrecy and reenforces this silence. The harm of this process, a process that utterly precludes speech, then becomes all of a piece. If there is no right place to go to say, this hurt me, then a woman is simply the one who can be treated this way, and no harm, as they say, is done.

In point of fact, I would prefer not to have to spend all this energy getting the law to recognize wrongs to women as wrong. But it seems to be necessary to legitimize our injuries as injuries in order to delegitimize our victimization by them, without which it is difficult to move in more positive ways. The legal claim for sexual harassment made the events of sexual harassment illegitimate socially as well as legally for the first time. Let me know if you figure out a better way to do that.

At this interface between law and society, we need to remember what the legitimacy courts give they can also take. Compared with a possibility of relief where no possibility of relief existed, since women started out with nothing in this area, this worry seems a bit fancy. Whether the possibility of relief alters the terms of power that give rise to sexual harassment itself, which makes getting away with it possible, is a different problem. Sexual harassment, the legal claim, is a demand that state authority stand behind women's refusal of sexual access in certain situations that previously were a masculine prerogative. With sexism, there is always a risk that our demand for self-determination will be taken as a demand for paternal protection and will therefore strengthen male power rather than undermine it. This seems a particularly valid concern because the law of sexual harassment began as case law, without legislative guidance or definition.

Institutional support for sexual self-determination is a victory; institutional paternalism reinforces our lack of self-determination. The problem is, the state has never in fact protected women's dignity or bodily integrity. It just says it does. Its protections have been both condescending *and* unreal, in effect strengthening the protector's choice to violate the protected at will, whether the protector is the individual perpetrator or the state. This does not seem to me a reason not to have a law against sexual harassment. It is a reason to demand that the promise of "equal protection of the laws" be *delivered upon* for us, as it is when real people are violated. It is also part of a larger political struggle to value women more than the male pleasure of using us is valued. Ultimately, though, the question of whether the use of the state for women helps or hurts can be answered only in practice, because so little real protection of the laws has ever been delivered.

The legal claim for sexual harassment marks the first time in history, to my knowledge, that women have defined women's injuries in a law. Consider what has happened with rape. We have never defined the injury of rape; men define it. The men who define it, define what they take to be this violation of women according to, among other things, what they think they don't do. In this way rape becomes an act of a stranger (they mean Black) committed upon a woman (white) whom he has never seen before. Most rapes are intraracial and are committed by men the women know. Ask a woman if she has ever been raped, and often she says, "Well . . . not really." In that silence between the well and the not really, she just measured what happened to her against every rape case she ever heard about and decided she would lose in court. Es-

> *"Sexual abuse mutes victims socially through the violation itself."*

pecially when you are part of a subordinated group, your own definition of your injuries is powerfully shaped by your assessment of whether you could get anyone to do anything about it, including anything official. You are realistic by necessity, and the voice of law is the voice in power. When the design of a legal wrong does not fit the wrong as it happens to you, as is the case with rape, that law can undermine your social and political as well as legal legitimacy in saying that what happened was an injury at all—even to yourself.

It is never too soon to worry about this, but it may be too soon to know whether the law against sexual harassment will be taken away from us or turn into nothing or turn ugly in our hands. The fact is, this law is working surprisingly well for women by any standards, particularly when compared with the rest of sex discrimination law. If the question is whether a law designed from women's standpoint and administered through this legal system can do anything for women—which always seems to me to be a good question—this experience so far gives a qualified and limited yes.

It is hard to unthink what you know, but there was a time when the facts that amount to sexual harassment did not amount to sexual harassment. It is a bit like the injuries of pornography until recently. The facts amounting to the harm did not socially "exist," had no shape, no cognitive coherence; far less did they state a legal claim. It just happened to you. To the women to whom it happened, it wasn't part of anything, much less something big or shared like gender. It fit no known pattern. It was neither a regularity nor an irregularity. Even social scientists didn't study it, and they study anything that moves. When law recognized sexual harassment as a practice of sex discrimination, it moved it from the realm of "and then he . . . and then he . . . ," the primitive language in which sexual abuse lives inside a woman, into an experience with a form, an etiology, a cumulativeness—as well as a club.

The shape, the positioning, and the club—each is equally crucial politically. Once it became possible to do something about sexual harassment, it became possible to know more about it, because it became possible for its victims to speak about it. Now we know, as we did not when it first became illegal, that this problem is commonplace. We know this not just because it has to be true, but as documented fact. Between a quarter and a third of women in the federal workforce report having been sexually harassed, many physically, at least once in the last two years. Projected, that becomes 85 percent of all women at some point in their working lives. This figure is based on asking women "Have you ever been sexually harassed?"—the conclusion—not "has this fact happened? has that fact happened?" which usually produces more. The figures for sexual harassment of students are comparable.

When faced with individual incidents of sexual harassment, the legal system's first question was, is it a personal episode? Legally, this was a way the courts inquired into whether the incidents were based on sex, as they had to be to be sex discrimination. Politically, it was a move to isolate victims by stigmatizing them as deviant. It also seemed odd to me that a relationship was either personal or gendered, meaning that one is not a woman personally. Statistical frequency alone does not make an event not personal, of course, but the presumption that sexual pressure in contexts of unequal power is an isolated idiosyncrasy to unique individual victims has been undermined both by the numbers and by their division by gender. Overwhelmingly, it is men who sexually harass women, a lot of them. Actually, it is even more accurate to say that men do this than to say that women have this done to them. This is a description of the perpetrators' behavior, not of the statisticians' feminism.

> *"The legal claim for sexual harassment marks the first time in history . . . that women have defined women's injuries in a law."*

Sexual harassment has also emerged as a creature of hierarchy. It inhabits what I call hierarchies among men: arrangements in which some men are below other men, as in employer/employee and teacher/student. In workplaces, sexual harassment by supervisors of subordinates is common; in education, by administrators of lower-level administrators, by faculty of students. But it also happens among coworkers, from third parties, even by subordinates in the workplace, men who are women's hierarchical inferiors or peers. Basically, it is done by men to women regardless of relative position on the formal hierarchy. I believe that the reason sexual harassment was first established as an injury of the systematic abuse of power in hierarchies among men is that this is power men recognize. They comprehend from personal experience that something is held over your head if you do not comply. The lateral or reverse hierarchical examples suggest something beyond this, something men don't understand from personal experience because they take its advantages for granted: gender is also a hierarchy. The courts do not use this analysis, but some act as though they understand it.

Sex discrimination law had to adjust a bit to accommodate the realities of sexual harassment. Like many other injuries of gender, it wasn't written for this. For something to be based on gender in the legal sense means it happens to a woman as a woman, not as an individual. Membership in a gender is understood as the opposite of, rather than part of, individuality. Clearly, sexual harassment is one of the last situations in which a woman is treated without regard to her sex; it is because of her sex that it happens. But the social meaning attributed to women as a class, in which women are defined as gender female by sexual accessibility to men, is not what courts have considered before when they have determined whether a given incident occurred because of sex. . . .

> *"Once it became possible to do something about sexual harassment, it became possible to know more about it."*

Once sexual harassment was established as bigger than personal, the courts' next legal question was whether it was smaller than biological. To say that sexual harassment was biological seemed to me a very negative thing to say about men, but defendants seemed to think it precluded liability. Plaintiffs argued that sexual harassment is not biological in that men who don't do it have nothing wrong with their testosterone levels. Besides, if murder were found to have biological correlates, it would still be a crime. Thus, although the question purported to be whether the acts were based on sex, the implicit issue seemed to be whether the source of the impetus for doing the acts was relevant to their harmfulness.

Similarly structured was the charge that women who resented sexual harassment were oversensitive. Not that the acts did not occur, but rather that it was unreasonable to experience them as harmful. Such a harm would be based not on sex but on individual hysteria. Again shifting the inquiry away from whether the acts are based on sex in the guise of pursuing it, away from whether they occurred to whether it should matter if they did, the question became whether the acts were properly harmful. Only this time it was not the perpetrator's drives that made him not liable but the target's sensitivity that made the acts not a harm at all. It was pointed out that too many people are victimized by sexual harassment to consider them all hysterics. Besides, in other individual injury law, victims are not blamed; perpetrators are required to take victims as they find them, so long as they are not supposed to be doing what they are doing.

> *"Sex discrimination law had to adjust a bit to accommodate the realities of sexual harassment."*

Once these excuses were rejected, then it was said that sexual harassment was not really an employment-related problem. That became hard to maintain when it was her job the woman lost. If it was, in fact, a personal relationship, it apparently did not start and stop there, although this is also a question of proof, leaving the true meaning of the events to trial. The perpetrator may have thought it was all affectionate or friendly or fun, but the victim experienced it as hateful, dangerous, and damaging. Results in such cases have been mixed. Some judges have accepted the perpetrator's view; for instance, one judge held queries by the defendant such as "What am I going to get for this?" and repeated importunings to "go out" to be "susceptible of innocent interpretation." Other judges, on virtually identical facts, for example, "When are you going to do something nice for me?" have held for the plaintiff. For what it's worth, the judge in the first case was a man, in the second a woman.

That sexual harassment is sex-based discrimination seems to be legally established, at least for now. In one of the few cases that reported litigating the issue of sex basis, defendants argued that a sex-based claim was not stated when a woman worker complained of terms of abuse directed at her at work such as "slut," "bitch," and "fucking cunt" and "many sexually oriented drawings posted on pillars and at other conspicuous places around the warehouse" with plaintiffs' initials on them, presenting her having sex with an animal. The court said: "[T]he sexually offensive conduct and language used would have been almost irrelevant and would have failed entirely in its crude purpose had the plaintiff been a man. I do not hesitate to find that but for her sex, the plaintiff would not have been subjected to the harassment she suffered." "Obvious" or "patently obvious" they often call it. I guess this is what it looks like to have proven a point.

Sexual harassment was first recognized as an injury of gender in what I called incidents of quid pro quo. Sometimes people think that harassment has to be constant. It doesn't; it's a term of art in which once can be enough. Typically, an advance is made, rejected, and a loss follows. For a while it looked as if this three-step occurrence was in danger of going from one form in which sexual harassment can occur into a series of required hurdles. In many situations the woman is forced to submit instead of being able to reject the advance. The problem has become whether, say, being forced into intercourse at work will be seen as a failed quid pro quo or as an instance of sexual harassment in which the forced sex constitutes the injury.

I know of one reported case in employment and one in education in which women who were forced to submit to the sex brought a sexual harassment claim against the perpetrator; so far only the education case has won on the facts. The employment case that lost on the facts was reversed on appeal. The pressures for sex were seen to state a claim without respect to the fact that the woman was not able to avoid complying. It is unclear if the unwanted advances constitute a claim, separate and apart from whether or not they are able to be resisted, which they should; or if the acts of forced sex would also constitute an environmental claim separate from any quid pro quo, as it seems to me they also should. In the education case, the case of Paul Mann, the students were allowed to recover punitive damages for the forced sex. If sexual harassment is not to be defined only as sexual attention imposed upon someone who is not in a position to refuse it, who refuses it, women who are forced to submit to sex must be understood as harmed not less, but as much or more, than those who are able to make their refusals effective. . . .

> *"Too many people are victimized by sexual harassment to consider them all hysterics."*

Most victims of sexual harassment, if the incidence data are correct, never file complaints. Many who are viciously violated are so ashamed to make that violation public that they submit in silence, although it devastates their self-respect and often their health, or they leave the job without complaint, although it threatens their survival and that of their families. If, on top of the cost of making the violation known, which is painful enough, they know that the entire range of their sexual experiences, attitudes, preferences, and practices are to be discoverable, few such actions will be brought, no matter how badly the victims are hurt. Faced with a choice between forced sex in their jobs or schools on the one hand and forced sexual disclosure for the public record on the other, few will choose the latter. This cruel paradox would effectively eliminate much progress in this area.

Put another way, part of the power held by perpetrators of sexual harassment is the threat of making the sexual abuse public knowledge. This functions like blackmail in silencing the victim and allowing the abuse to continue. It is a fact that public knowledge of sexual abuse is often worse for the abused than the abuser, and victims who choose to complain have the courage to take that on. To add to their burden the potential of making public their entire personal life, information that has no relation to the fact or severity of the incidents complained of, is to make the law of this area implicitly complicit in the blackmail that keeps victims from exercising their rights and to enhance the impunity of perpetrators. In effect, it means open season on anyone who does not want her entire intimate life available to public scrutiny. In other contexts such private information has been found intrusive, irrelevant, and more prejudicial than probative. To allow it to be discovered in the sexual harassment area amounts to a requirement that women be further violated in order to be permitted to seek relief for having been violated. I also will never understand why a violation's severity, or even its likelihood of occurrence, is measured according to the character of the violated, rather than by what was done to them.

> *"In many situations the woman is forced to submit instead of being able to reject the advance."*

In most reported sexual harassment cases, especially rulings on law more than on facts, the trend is almost uniformly favorable to the development of this claim. At least, so far. This almost certainly does not represent social reality. It may not even reflect most cases in litigation. And there may be conflicts building, for example, between those who value speech in the abstract more than they value people in the concrete. Much of sexual harassment is words. Women are called "cunt," "pussy," "tits"; they are invited to a company party with "bring your own bathing suits (women, either half)"; they confront their tormentor in front of their manager with, "You have called me a fucking bitch," only to be answered, "No, I didn't. I called you a fucking cunt." One court issued an injunction against inquiries such as "Did you get any over the weekend?" One case holds that where "a person in a position to grant or withhold employment opportunities uses that authority to attempt to induce workers and job seekers to submit to sexual advances, prostitution, and pornographic entertainment, and boasts of an ability to intimidate those who displease him," sexual harassment (and intentional infliction of emotional distress) are pleaded. Sexual harassment can also include pictures; visual as well as verbal pornography is commonly used as part of the abuse. Yet one judge found, apparently as a matter of law, that the pervasive presence of pornography in the workplace did not constitute an unreasonable work environment because, "For better or worse, modern America features open displays of written and pictorial erotica. Shopping centers, candy stores and prime time television regularly display naked bodies and erotic real or simulated sex acts. Living in this milieu, the average American should not be legally offended by sexually explicit posters." She did not say she was offended, she said she was discriminated against based on her sex. If the pervasiveness of an abuse makes it nonactionable, no inequality sufficiently institutionalized to merit a law against it would be actionable.

Further examples of this internecine conflict have arisen in education. At the

Massachusetts Institute of Technology pornography used to be shown every year during registration. Is this *not* sexual harassment in education, as a group of women complained it was, because attendance is voluntary, both sexes go, it is screened in groups rather than individually, nobody is directly propositioned, and it is pictures and words? Or is it sexual harassment because the status and treatment of women, supposedly secured from sex-differential harm, are damaged, including that of those who do not attend, which harms individuals and undermines sex equality; therefore pictures and words are the media through which the sex discrimination is accomplished?

> *"When we started, there was absolutely no judicial precedent for allowing a sex discrimination suit for sexual harassment."*

For feminist jurisprudence, the sexual harassment attempt suggests that if a legal initiative is set up right from the beginning, meaning if it is designed from women's real experience of violation, it can make some difference. To a degree women's experience can be written into law, even in some tension with the current doctrinal framework. Women who want to resist their victimization with legal terms that imagine it is not inevitable can be given some chance, which is more than they had before. Law is not everything in this respect, but it is not nothing either. Perhaps the most important lesson is that the mountain can be moved. When we started, there was absolutely no judicial precedent for allowing a sex discrimination suit for sexual harassment. Sometimes even the law does something for the first time.

Current Sexual Harassment Definitions Harm Women

by Sarah J. McCarthy

About the author: *Sarah J. McCarthy is a restaurateur and writer.*

On the same day that Ted Kennedy asked forgiveness for his personal "short-comings," he advocated slapping lottery-size punitive damages on small-business owners who may be guilty of excessive flirting, or whose employees may be guilty of talking dirty. Senator Kennedy expressed regrets that the new civil rights bill caps punitive damages for sexual harassment as high as $300,000 (depending on company size), and he promises to push for increases next year. Note that the senators have voted to exempt themselves from punitive damages.

I am the owner of a small restaurant/bar that employs approximately 20 young males whose role models range from Axl Rose to John Belushi. They work hard in a high-stress, fast-paced job in a hot kitchen and at times they are guilty of colorful language. They have also been overheard telling Pee-Wee Herman jokes and listening to obnoxious rock lyrics. They have discussed pornography and they have flirted with waitresses. One chef/manager has asked out a pretty blonde waitress probably 100 times in three years. She seems to enjoy the game, but always says no. Everyone calls everyone else "Honey"—it's a ritual, a way of softening what sound like barked orders: "I need the medium-rare shish kebab *now!*"

The Feminist Gestapo

"Honey" doesn't mean the same thing here as it does in women's studies departments or at the EEOC [Equal Employment Opportunity Commission]. The auto body shop down the street has pinups. Perhaps under the vigilant eyes of the feminist political correctness gestapo we can reshape our employees' behavior so they act more like nerds from the Yale women's studies department. The gestapo will not lack for potential informers seeking punitive damages and instant riches.

With the Civil Rights Bill of 1991 we are witnessing the most organized and systematic assault on free speech and privacy since the McCarthy era. The vagueness of the sexual harassment law, combined with our current litigation explosion, is a frightening prospect for small businesses. We are now financially responsible for sexually offensive verbal behavior, even if we don't know it is occurring, under a law that provides no guidelines to define "offensive" and "harassment." This is a cultural fascism unmatched since the Chinese communists outlawed hand-holding, decorative clothing and premarital sex.

This law is detrimental even to the women it professes to help. I am a feminist, but the law has made me fearful of hiring women. If one of our cooks or managers—or my husband or sons—offends someone, it could cost us $100,000 in punitive damages and legal expenses. There will be no insurance fund or stockholders or taxpayers to pick up the tab.

Harming Feminism

When I was a feminist activist in the Seventies, we knew the dangers of a pedestal—it was said to be as confining as any other small place. As we were revolted and outraged by the woman-hatred in violent pornography, we reminded each other that education, not laws, was the solution to our problems. In Women Against Sexist Violence in Pornography and Media, in Pittsburgh, we were well aware of the dangers of encroaching on the First Amendment. Free speech was, perhaps more than anything else, what made our country grow into a land of enlightenment and diversity. The lesbians among us were aware that the same laws used to censor pornography could be used against them if their sexual expressions were deemed offensive.

We admired powerful women writers such as Marge Piercy and poets like Robin Morgan who swooped in from nowhere, writing break-your-chains poems about women swinging from crystal chandeliers like monkey vines and defecating in punch bowls. Are we allowed to talk about these poems in the current American workplace?

The lawyers—the prim women and men who went to the politically correct law schools—believe with

> *"This law is detrimental even to the women it professes to help."*

sophomoric arrogance that the solution to all the world's problems is tort litigation. We now have eternally complicated questions of sexual politics judged by the shifting standards of the reasonable prude.

To the leadership of the women's movement: You do women a disservice. You ladies—and I use that term intentionally—have trivialized the women's movement. You have made us ladies again. You have not considered the unintended effects of your sexual harassment law. You are saying that too many things men say and do with each other are too rough-and-tumble for us. Wielding the power of your $300,000 lawsuits, you are frightening managers into hiring men over women. I know that I am so frightened. You have installed a double pane of glass on the glass ceiling with the help of your white knight and protector, Senator Kennedy.

You and your allies tried to lynch Clarence Thomas. You alienate your natural allies. Men and women who wanted to work shoulder to shoulder with you are now looking over their shoulders. You have made women into china dolls that if broken come with a $300,000 price tag. The games, intrigue, nuances and fun of flirting have been made into criminal activity.

We women are not as delicate and powerless as you think. We do not want victim status in the workplace. Don't try to foist it on us.

Legal Definitions of Sexual Harassment Are Too Broad

by Lloyd R. Cohen

About the author: *Lloyd R. Cohen is an associate professor of law at Chicago-Ken College of Law. He has written and lectured widely on questions of ethics and law.*

At the mention of the term sexual harassment, I feel the intellectual ground give way beneath my feet. Sexual harassment is a term that has, like fascist and racist, some intellectual content and strong pejorative implication, but lacks a clear definition. As in the case of the other two terms, it is not by accident that the definition of sexual harassment has become more, rather than less, elusive with use.

Deliberate Misinterpretations

The problem is not simply that the ordinary language meaning of the phrase is insufficiently narrow and precise to capture the activities it is meant to cover. Another important source of difficulty is that, as with many politicized phrases, sexual harassment is deliberately employed loosely and imprecisely. The term connotes a social and legal wrong, and invites being employed as a broad brush to tar behavior to which a speaker objects even if the audience might not. Sexual banter, displaying *Playboy* centerfolds, requests for sex in exchange for job promotions, and rape can all be lumped together as sexual harassment. If the label sticks, the former acts will be tainted by the latter.

It makes a thoughtful person uneasy when a term that is intended to have moral, social, and legal consequences is bandied about without an implicit or explicit definition. When someone uses the term sexual harassment, it is unclear (1) what class of behavior the speaker implicitly wishes to condemn; and (2) what social and legal consequences are expected to flow from that condemnation. While some forms of sexual harassment need to be punished and stigmatized, I distrust the use of a category that seems too broad at both ends. Rape, sexual assault, and obscene phone calls could all be described as sexual harassment. But to what purpose? No new legal, social, or moral category is needed to cover these offenses. There is virtual unanimity that they are always and everywhere bad acts, and are consequently both tortious and criminal. Arguably the legal remedies available to attack such behavior are for one reason or other less than optimally effective. But the brouhaha about sexual harassment is not about crafting new remedies for old wrongs, but of recognizing new wrongs. At the other end of the spectrum, some of those most vociferous in raising the specter of sexual harassment use the label to cover acts that the rest of us view as relatively innocent, e.g., admiring the female physique or suggesting that men and women have fundamentally different interests and abilities.

Narrowing the Definition

For the purpose of this discussion, a preliminary definition, that may be overly broad but represents an ordinary language interpretation of the words, will serve as a starting point. Sexual harassment is any unwelcome tactile, visual, or verbal communication of a sexual nature. As broad as this definition may appear it fails to cover some acts which have been labeled as sexual harassment, for example, the hiring of a striptease artist by a college fraternity. Three questions about sexual harassment need to be explored: (1) Is everything that falls within the definition evil and should it be condemned? (2) Is sexual harassment a class of behavior that is well suited to legal regulation? (3) Have recent legal assaults on this behavior been well aimed? The prevailing view implicitly answers each of these questions in the affirmative. Whether these answers are correct or not, for the sake of argument and because the conventional wisdom is still unexamined, the opposing perspective will be presented in the hope of generating more critical discourse.

Some claims of sexual harassment arise from the fact that men's tastes are different than women's. This is not to say that men and women do not differ among themselves, but certain kinds of behavior are more characteristically male and others more characteristically female. Men talk more often about sports while women discuss clothes; men read magazines like *Popular Mechanics* while women prefer *Good Housekeeping*. Such dif-

> *"Sexual harassment is a term that . . . lacks a clear definition."*

ferences usually result in little more than men and women being bored or uneasy when forced into the company of a group of the opposite sex. Most of the sources of this discomfort could not reasonably be labeled as sexual harassment.

Some types of behavior based on gender differences are of an erotic or quasi-erotic nature. Many men enjoy looking at pictures of naked women. Women seem to have less interest in looking at the naked bodies of either men or women. Men are more inclined to make sexual references in their speech and to tell off-color jokes, and more importantly to feel free doing this in a wider variety of social settings. Some women will find such discussions and language offensive and unpleasant, and here, because the discomfort is related to the erotic character of the activity, the sexual harassment label may apply.

Is Sexual Harassment Benign or Evil?

Are there unwelcome sexual communications that do not rise to the level of a wrong? And do all communications that rise to that level simultaneously also rise to the level of tort? If so, then what lies in between will be a null set. Rather than discuss sexual harassment in the abstract, it will be more enlightening to examine the issue in light of concrete examples describing possibly unwelcome sexual communication. Two incidents, drawn from my family history, one involving my great-grandmother and the other myself, will serve as illustrations.

My great-grandfather was a renowned Orthodox rabbi in Lithuania and, after about 1925, in Philadelphia. Some time in the 1930s, his youngest daughter was betrothed to an Orthodox man. When my great-grandmother, a pious woman in her fifties, attempted to shake hands with her future son-in-law, he pulled away and objected that he would touch no woman other than his wife. Admittedly this man's behavior was extreme even by Orthodox standards, but his reaction was honest and reflected his religious beliefs. The prospect of touching a woman other than his wife, even in such an innocent and harmless manner, was offensive. To this man my great-grandmother's outstretched hand was a form of sexual harassment. From a very different portion of the social spectrum, I offer a personal experience. Shortly after I graduated from college I worked for a New York insurance company. One morning a young married woman employee with whom I had had no prior romantic relationship, literally pulled me into an office closet for a bit of sexual play. Some people in my position would have undoubtedly been outraged by the lady's behavior—I was not. I found her communication anything but unwelcome.

"Some of those most vociferous in raising the specter of sexual harassment use the label to cover acts that the rest of us view as relatively innocent."

These incidents are not meant to be illustrative of all, most, or even many incidents of alleged sexual harassment. They differ most importantly from the core case in that the putative harasser in both cases was a woman and the victim was a man. Instead they are meant to show that the contours of appropriate behavior between the sexes, either as a prelude to, or part of, a sexual relationship, or simply as an aspect of ordinary social discourse are not a fixed, universally known, or widely shared set of rules. And, to the extent that there are such rules there are a variety of views as to how they apply in different social environments. Even those who agree on where to draw the lines between the acceptable and the unacceptable will dispute whether violation of these rules should be treated as a faux pas, extremely gauche behavior, a tort, or a crime.

> *"Some claims of sexual harassment arise from the fact that men's tastes are different than women's."*

What social or legal rule makes sense in response to this cognitive, aesthetic, and ethical dispersion? A widely shared view of a liberal society has it that private acts between consenting adults are not the concern of society or the state. If a man's sexually aggressive behavior is accepted or approved of by the woman toward whom it is directed most of us would find no social and, *a fortiori*, no legal wrong. If a woman does not welcome a man's sexually aggressive behavior and he knows it and persists in it, he is guilty of at least a social wrong, and if his behavior is egregious enough, a legal one as well. Were this the whole world of possibilities, the social resolution, though perhaps not the legal one, would be easy enough. The first category would be permitted, the second would be condemned. . . .

Sexual Communication

Since sexual communication is such an important aspect of life, and takes place in the shadow of legal and social rules, even small changes in the rules can have a great impact on people's lives. If women and men are too fearful of contact with the opposite sex, the social preliminaries to romantic union may never occur. These are not idle or unfounded speculations. The market for romantic partners is a daunting one. We all know of men and women who, although they very much want to find a romantic partner, are counseled by their fears more than by their hopes, and so never make the leaps necessary to achieve their goal.

In traditional societies, and even in traditional corners of our own, there are well known, standard forms of courtship. Whether it is the use of a matchmaker or some other social device, people who grew up within a particular culture know the path they must tread. For most contemporary Americans these traditional forms are part of a charming ethnic heritage rather than a viable possibility.

In our open, dynamic, and multi-cultural society there is no one, or even a discrete, set of accepted ways in which men and women can make known their general availability, to say nothing of their attraction to a particular person. The dance of courtship is no longer a minuet, if it ever was. It is more like the variety of gyrations one might observe in a discothèque; there are no commonly shared steps. Acceptable sexual conduct covers the field from my great aunt's husband to my co-worker of twenty-two years ago, and beyond. Sometimes we manage to signal sexual values through, dress, occupation, location or activity, but often we do not. Prudes and prostitutes are forced to rub shoulders with one another, usually without visual signals of the values embodied in those shoulders. So, we continually confront the two-sided danger of either acting too aggressively, with all the attendant social and legal costs, or, of acting too diffidently or not at all, and thereby losing an opportunity for a relationship. For those at the social extremes, the dance may be easiest; they know their steps. For those in the vast middle ground looking in both directions at the same time, the dance of courtship is more daunting. Learning the steps well enough to avoid stepping on, or tripping over, one's partner's feet is challenge enough. To do this under the threat of legal sanctions for overly aggressive but non-tortious behavior will drive men from the dance floor, and make it that much more difficult for men and women to find partners.

Standards of Behavior and the Law

The plea for recognition of, and sensitivity to, the delicate social institution we are affecting should not be interpreted as a call for no regulation of unwelcome sexual communication. Rather, it is a call for recognition of the benefits as well as the costs of aggressive sexual communication and for giving them proper weight in social and legal rules. It is seemingly natural to treat one's own standards of behavior as the appropriate legal and social norm. But a spirit of, if not complete, but at least of heightened legal, if not social, tolerance toward other people's communication is urgently needed. For some men, crude conversation is more natural and common—and not all women are put off by it. Different people have different tastes, and different social settings have different standards of accepted behavior. It is all too tempting to fall into a grand ethnocentrism in which the standards of our class, our generation, our religion, our social context, and our region are taken to be the standard of behavior for the whole society, and to seek to impose it on all through legislation.

> *"A widely shared view of a liberal society has it that private acts between consenting adults are not the concern of society or the state."*

Law is a vital tool of social regulation. Were it not for the very existence of law, and the reasonable set of property, contract, tort, and criminal rights and duties that it enforces, this nation would not be the rich, free, and generally pleasant place it is. Yet recognizing that law is on balance a fine thing does not mean that every aspect of life should be regulated by that institution.

Law, like all social institutions, has its strengths and weaknesses. Discussion of legal issues frequently takes place with the tacit assumption that law works costlessly, instantaneously, and with perfect accuracy. Were this assumption made explicit, no one would likely assent to it. But since the transaction costs of law are generally not explicitly modeled, discussion of legal reform is often carried on with the implicit assumption that costs are negligible and may be ignored. Thus for some commentators the question of whether to provide legal sanctions against a particular behavior collapses into determining whether that behavior is bad. The fact is that the law is a costly, inaccurate, and slow institution of social regulation and the remedies it offers are frequently unenforceable and not well tied to the wrong to be remedied. Even if it were possible theoretically to define a category of sexual harassment as evil, it may still not be sensible to impose legal sanctions on such behavior.

Sexual Harassment in the Workplace

Sexual harassment is an emerging legal category. Its current place in the legal architecture may be temporary or it may expand with time. Current federal prohibitions against sexual harassment derive from Section 703 of Title VII of the 1964 Civil Rights Act, which prohibits workplace discrimination based on sex. A series of cases culminating with *Meritor Savings Bank v. Vinson*, found that certain forms of sexual harassment constituted prohibited sex discrimination.

> *"Law, like all social institutions, has its strengths and weaknesses."*

There are three interesting questions about the legal standards that have thus far developed: (1) Are the appropriate parties being held liable? (2) Are the standards of liability sensible? (3) Is the workplace a particularly fruitful area to regulate?

Sexual harassment suits fall into two categories referred to in the legal literature as *quid pro quo* and "hostile environment." Under the first category the complainant asserts that because the sexual communication originates from the employee's supervisor, submission to unwelcome sexual communication is an express or implied condition of employment. The second category covers all other forms of unwelcome sexual communication in the workplace. The distinction between these two categories is important because it is tied to the most curious and suspect aspects of the law of sexual harassment, the designation of the employer as a defendant in the suit, and the standards of liability under which he will be judged. In virtually all sexual harassment cases the employer is made a party to the action and when liability is found, it is the employer who must foot the bill.

Because of its more liberal standards for establishing employer liability, *quid pro quo* cases are far more popular with plaintiffs than hostile environment cases. In a hostile environment case the complainant must show that the employer had notice of the hostile environment and failed to respond adequately. Notice is not identical with knowledge. If the employer knew or should have known of the harassment, that will be sufficient. In a *quid pro quo* case no such notice is required. The unwelcome sexual communication of a supervisor will be imputed to the employer. The employer cannot escape liability even if he had no way of knowing of the harassing behavior and had in place a strictly enforced policy against sexual harassment.

> *"To the extent that employers fear sexual harassment suits, they will be inclined to draw the borders of acceptable male-female communication narrowly."*

The employer's liability for an employee's sins is known as vicarious liability, which is a common feature of law. What makes it a peculiar, indeed a unique, application in the case of sexual harassment is that normally it is only employed when the acts of an employee are intended to serve the business interests of the employer. In the case of sexual harassment, the harassing behavior is not merely orthogonal to the employer's interest, but actually adverse to it. Let us assume that the employer is unaware of the harassment. The sexual harasser obviously attaches some positive value to the activity, and, equally obviously, his victims attach a negative value to it. Yet this is not merely a two person game. Harassment costs that initially fall on the firm's female employees do not stop there. They will be passed on to the employer in the form of higher turnover rates, greater difficulty in filling positions at otherwise competitive wages, and a less productive working environment. The employer must ultimately pay the price of the harassment even if he is not legally liable.

Punishment

What if the employer is aware of the harassment? Could he not and would he not at least reduce the harasser's income to reflect the psychic benefit the latter is receiving? While this is a theoretical possibility, the cost saving is unlikely to be sufficient to make up for the losses from the turnover of female employees. It is hard to imagine a situation in which the right to harass is financially more valuable to the harasser than the cost to the victim. Permitting male employees to use the workplace as a site to torment female employees with unwelcome sexual communication will always be a net cost to employers.

Aside from the unfairness of imposing liability on the employer for the harassment of one employee by another, a more important question is whether such liability conveys the appropriate incentives. Assuming that the behavior being prohibited is indeed something evil that should be legally prohibited and eliminated, this form of action is placing vicarious liability on the employer, who is the appropriate agent for optimally controlling this behavior.

At first blush vicarious liability seems an inefficient remedy in that it makes one of the wronged parties, rather than the wrongdoer, pay for the wrong to the other. It seems as though the employer must in effect pay twice for a wrong that was committed by the harasser, who pays nothing. This seemingly bizarre result will be partially mitigated by the employer's imposing some of the costs on the harassing employee, principally by dismissing him.

Even with this partial mitigation, the employer may be given too much incentive to deter harassment and may become overzealous. If the employer could costlessly and completely monitor all behavior in the workplace, and had a clear and precise definition of sexual harassment, he could prohibit all types of offensive behavior. But the world is not such a neat and clean place. Employers are generally not able to regulate the subtle and private behavior of their employees and, in this area, will be unsure of what to regulate. In the *Meritor* case, the Supreme Court, though willing to condemn sexual harassment, was loath to inform the world of the boundaries of this elusive cause of action. To the extent that employers fear sexual harassment suits, they will be inclined to draw the borders of acceptable male-female communication narrowly in order to distance their workplace environment from the invisible border of sexual harassment.

Workplace Problems

The workplace is an area where enforcement of laws against sexual harassment may yield great benefits. Time spent on the job takes up a good portion of most people's lives. Women invest a great deal of firm specific human capital in their jobs and will incur substantial transaction costs if they must change jobs. Ensuring that women are not the subject of on-the-job sexual harassment will eliminate the possibility that they will be compelled to change jobs and suffer large losses because of sexual harassment. Before concluding that legal regulation is warranted, one must inquire into the marginal benefits of a legal remedy and of its potential costs. Although it is clear that eliminating sexual harassment in the workplace offers real gains, one wonders why the market has not already substantially eliminated it. Precisely because sexual harassment imposes costs on

> *"It is hard to see how true large-scale sexual harassment in the workplace can survive a market test."*

employers that will ultimately be shifted to the harasser, it is hard to see how true large-scale sexual harassment in the workplace can survive a market test.

In support of this proposition, the results of a sifting of the records of harassment cases indicate that a grossly disproportionate number of sexual harassment suits come from public sector employment. Since government employers do not face the market constraints of private employers and have less discretion in dismissing employees, they have less incentive and ability to discipline sexual harassment.

Still, even in a well functioning employment market some women are likely to be outraged by the sexual communications of fellow employees. Some of this will be sexual harassment, but perhaps some will not. The world of work is a congeries of different social settings. A woman can find employment everywhere from a Nevada whorehouse to a convent. From a sexual communication perspective is it reasonable to expect or to impose the same standards of behavior on each of these jobs and all those in between? Obviously not. While identifying one firm as a Brooklyn spice importer and another as a Manhattan real estate manager may not yield a clue as to the standards of sexual communication each expects and accepts from its employees, it is not unreasonable that they might differ on this continuum. In a free market both employers and employees can sort themselves on this social dimension as well as on all others. Some behavior that might otherwise appear as sexual harassment may be better viewed as a temporary mis-sorting of people in the employment market.

The greatest cost to regulating sexual harassment in the workplace is that for an increasing number of people the workplace represents by far the best avenue for finding and pursuing romantic interests. In our modern, open, dynamic society there are all too few social situations where men and women can meet and participate in the market for romantic partners without suffering this as the central purpose of the activity. At work they can flirt and in other ways get the ball rolling in a controlled, largely non-threatening environment. Should this marketplace be substantially damaged by regulations, the lives of those affected will be diminished. They will have more difficulty finding partners and will have to search in less attractive places.

Current Laws Should Be Enforced

This article reflects my scepticism about the social and legal category of sexual harassment and it may convey the sense that the law should bend over backwards to avoid entering this arena. This is not so. No argument is made for the abolition or curtailment of enforcement of traditional criminal and tort penalties for sexual offenses. On the contrary, they should be enforced more vigorously and be punished more harshly. Men, being stronger and more aggressive than women, can—and some men will—take great advantage of them under the guise of ambiguous communication. We have a legal and social obligation to prevent or punish such behavior. But creating the undefined, politicized category of sexual harassment seems a poorly aimed and dangerous way to go about it.

175

Broad Legal Definitions of Sexual Harassment Threaten Men

by John Leo

About the author: *John Leo is an editorialist for the weekly newsmagazine* U.S. News & World Report.

What have we learned in our one-week crash course on sexual harassment? Well, we now know that a great many men are surprised to learn that a great many women are furious over constant sexual hassles, large and small, that demean women and hold them back at work. "They just don't get it" was surely one of the most common phrases of the week. This roar of anger, accompanied by a vast outpouring of personal revelations about harassment and humiliation, is a massive political fact that sets the stage for the first wave of reform not directly prodded by the courts.

No Clear Definition

All this is to the good. The obvious power plays against women—sexual demands from supervisors and "hostile environments" designed to make women feel inferior and off balance—are clearly understood and clearly illegal. Beyond that, there is a good deal of confusion, and no one has been able to define sexual harassment very well. Judith Lichtman of the Women's Legal Defense Fund is impatient with this view, saying, "People may prefer to believe it's a murky subject. But that's baloney. . . . You don't have to be a genius to figure out that you're being harassed." Three inches away from this quote in the *Washington Post*, Staff Writer Kim Masters tells us that while working as a reporter she was genially propositioned by a bureaucrat several times. As Masters tells it—"He never hinted that he would try to hurt me professionally," and he continued to be a good source, giving her "all kinds of leads for stories." This was a case of sexual harassment, though it is hard to figure out why she thinks so.

Let us try to make the case for murk.

It is now accepted in the social sciences that males and females perceive verbal and nonverbal cues in different ways and therefore are exceptionally good at misunderstanding one another. This regularly produces Rashomon-like encounters, with each party aghast at the other's interpretation of what went on. Deborah Tannen's best-seller, *You Just Don't Understand*, demonstrates that the complaint of the week ("They just don't get it") works both ways in male-female conversations.

A Hostile Environment

Another source of confusion is that our conception of sexual harassment keeps expanding. The "hostile environment" ruling is a just one, but it means that all apparently innocent actions and comments might now be viewed as part of a pattern that injures women. One professor has been found guilty of the freshly minted offense of improper or unwelcome gazing. Consciousness-raising films indicate that a copy of *Playboy* lying about on a man's desk might come under the heading of harassment. A female worker in California was ordered to take down a photo calendar of men in bathing suits, lest some quibbling male make a harassment issue of it.

> *"A lot of males, guilty and innocent, are likely to be tainted by unsubstantiated charges."*

Some arguments against harassment sound as though the goal is to desexualize the workplace, but dating and courtship take place there. There is some evidence that young people are more dependent than ever on the workplace as a pool of potential mates. Is this wrong? If a woman says no to a request for a date, will a second request bring charges of harassment? No one knows. The use of the terms "unwanted" or "unwelcomed" sexual attention creates a Catch-22 for males, who rarely know whether a pitch will be "welcomed" until it's been made. It's almost impossible to read the sexual harassment literature without noticing its pinched view of sexuality as eroticized male power. (Law Prof. Catharine MacKinnon, the chief legal architect of our legal harassment policies, calls heterosexuality "the eroticization of dominance and submission.") As long as this view is buried in our policies, we will have trouble sorting out harassment issues.

Another strong tendency in the literature is the insistence that the law allow plaintiffs/victims to determine whether an offense has taken place. The courts have accepted this—the point of view of the victim is the point of view of the law. As one attorney for employers said: "If one woman's interpretation sets the legal standard, then it is virtually up to every woman in the workplace to define if she's been sexually harassed."

This puts sexual harassment in the same category as violations of college speech and behavior codes, which often turn on the feelings of the aggrieved rather than on any objective and definable offense. But if feelings are trumps, how do we know when sexism and harassment end and hypersensitivity begins?

The radical subjectivity that this places at the heart of harassment procedures makes for some curious arguments. At the University of Toronto, the suggestion that a third party be allowed to report incidents of harassment led to protests that only the plaintiff/victim—and not any corroborating witnesses—should have the prerogative of reporting and defining offenses.

Perhaps this decisive turn toward subjective determination of offenses was inevitable. It is certainly true that under the old objective, where's-the-evidence standard, few harassers were being punished. But it opens an era in which a lot of males, guilty and innocent, are likely to be tainted by unsubstantiated charges.

Sexual Harassment Definitions Discriminate Against Men

by Michael Weiss

About the author: *Michael Weiss is a fellow at the Texas Public Policy Foundation and an articles editor at the* Texas Law Review.

Clarence Thomas was nearly denied a seat on the U.S. Supreme Court because a woman who worked for him a decade ago said he had asked her out and discussed dirty movies with her. That's not the way the papers put it, of course. In the press, Thomas stood accused of "sexual harassment." By substituting that vague term for the specifics of Thomas's alleged behavior, reporters acknowledged a reality that became painfully clear during the grueling days of the Senate hearings on Anita Hill's charges: What was once merely obnoxious is now illegal.

Redefining Harassment

Catharine MacKinnon had a lot to do with that transformation. As a feminist legal scholar, she formulated a theory of sexual harassment that was adopted by the Supreme Court in 1986: Sexual harassment need not involve physical contact, the threat of retaliation, or even an intent to harass. It can consist merely of a "hostile" work environment, created by off-color jokes, nude pinups, inappropriate social interest, or anything else that might offend a woman's sensibilities. In this light, whether you think Anita Hill told the truth or not, Thomas's crime was all in her mind.

During the hearings, MacKinnon, now a University of Michigan law professor, took to the op-ed pages and the TV talk shows—including *Today*, *Donahue*, *Nightline*, and *Sonya Live*—to defend that standard and the ideas un-

Michael Weiss, "Crimes of the Head." Reprinted, with permission, from the January 1992 issue of *Reason* magazine. Copyright 1992 by the Reason Foundation, 3415 S. Sepulveda Blvd., Suite 400, Los Angeles, CA 90034.

derlying it. For the most part, she sounded quite moderate and reasonable, interested only in fairness and in vindicating the rights of working women. On *Nightline*, for example, she conceded that simple miscommunication underlies many cases of sexual harassment. MacKinnon's mainstream status was reflected by a flattering October 6 cover story in *The New York Times Magazine*. Later that month, Peter Jennings dubbed her "Person of the Week."

But there is another side to Catharine MacKinnon. Her writings and those of her allies confirm that the campaign against sexual harassment represents a radical departure from traditional notions of justice. Indeed, it is part of a broader attempt by feminist theorists to uproot fundamental legal principles that they view as perpetuating male domination of society. Those principles include such ostensibly gender-neutral concepts as consent, reasonableness, individual rights, and the presumption of innocence. The declared goal of the feminist jurisprudes is to transform the law from an instrument of subjugation into a system based on a woman's perspective.

Feminist Legal Theory

So far they appear to be succeeding. "Feminist legal theory is the most dynamic area of law today," writes Anastasia Toufexis in *Time*. "Feminist scholars have pioneered the concept of sexual harassment in the work place, catalyzed passage of rape shield laws and expanded the principle of self-defense to cover battered women accused of killing abusive mates."

Says Professor Cynthia F. Epstein of Stanford Law School, "Attorneys whose practice might be described as embracing or incorporating feminist jurisprudence have undoubtedly had a meaningful effect on modern law and public policy. Along with feminist practitioners, the legal theorists have addressed and affected the spheres of family law, employment law, criminal law, and first amendment law." Professor Laurence Tribe of Harvard Law School is also enthusiastic: "Over the next quarter century feminist legal theory is likely to be the most fertile source of important insights in the law."

What sort of insights does feminist jurisprudence offer? "The primary task of feminist scholars is to awaken women and men to the invidious ways in which patriarchy distorts all our lives," writes Leslie Bender, a professor at Syracuse University College of Law. Writing in *The Harvard Women's Law Journal*, Janet Rifkin defines patriarchy (others prefer the terms *androcentrism* or *phallocentrism*) as "any kind of group organization in which males hold dominant power and determine what part females shall and shall not play, and in which capacities assigned to women are relegated generally to the

> *"It is not enough to welcome women into the practical and political realms. Rather, those realms must be remade based on the female perspective."*

mystical and aesthetic, and excluded from the practical and political realms, these realms being regarded as separate and mutually exclusive."

Although Rifkin's definition draws on the narrow, anthropological meaning of the term, feminist scholars also use *patriarchy* more generally to describe any society based on the male perspective. To overcome patriarchy, it is not enough to welcome women into the practical and political realms. Rather, those realms must be remade based on the female perspective, as feminist theorists define it.

Exposing Patriarchy

The feminist jurisprudes seek to expose patriarchy as abstract, distanced, and repressive. They want to replace it with a new paradigm reflecting the experience of women, one based on context, relationship, and particulars. Female thinking, MacKinnon says, represents the "essential connectedness" of women, in contrast to the separateness of men. From the female perspective, all things are connected; diametric opposition—between mind and body, nature and culture, self and other, good and evil, personal and political—does not exist.

Yet feminist legal theory is built on the idea of a sharp male/female dichotomy. Hence some feminist jurisprudes distinguish between artificial dichotomies—those that men perceive—and natural dichotomies—those that women perceive. Other theorists, including MacKinnon, reject that approach. No one has been able to resolve the apparent contradiction between the idea that opposites are illusory and the idea that male thinking and female thinking are fundamentally opposed, at least not in terms that make sense by the standards of logic—but perhaps that's the point. Logic, after all, is a male concept.

> *"Some feminist jurisprudes distinguish between artificial dichotomies—those that men perceive—and natural dichotomies—those that women perceive."*

In the feminist vision, "care," a connection notion, replaces "rights," a separateness notion. "Male and female perceptions of value are not shared, and are perhaps not even perceptible to each other," writes Ann Scales of the University of New Mexico School of Law in the *Yale Law Journal*. (That is why, as we were reminded ad nauseum during the Thomas hearings, men "just don't get it.") "In our current genderized realm, therefore, the 'rights-based' and 'care-based' ethics cannot be blended. Those values cannot be content with multiplicity; they create the other and then devour it. Objectivity ignores context; reason is the opposite of emotion; rights preclude care."

In the context of sexual harassment, "care" requires that the law cast its net wide. Caring for women means protecting them not only from overt harassment but from feeling uncomfortable. In formulating her theory of sexual harassment in the mid-'70s, MacKinnon eschewed the traditional legal remedies of tort and contract. Although victims of sexual harassment could sue for assault and battery, intentional infliction of emotional distress, invasion of privacy, or intentional interference with a contract, MacKinnon deemed those approaches unsatisfactory. For one thing, under those remedies, a victim of sexual harassment could sue her employer only if she could show that he had authorized the harassment.

> *"Caring for women means protecting them not only from overt harassment but from feeling uncomfortable."*

More important, the standards that courts would use to determine whether any of those right violations had occurred would be based on the male perspective; male standards of behavior and male sensibilities would govern. MacKinnon believed that the ideas of tort and contract were "conceptually inadequate" because of "the social reality of men's sexual treatment of women." Since the main condition for sexual harassment is the social, economic, and political inequality of women, she argued, such actions are really a form of sex discrimination. In 1978, the U.S. Court of Appeals for the District of Columbia Circuit became the first appellate court to accept that argument.

In the 1986 case *Meritor Savings Bank v. Vinson*, which MacKinnon helped argue, the Supreme Court adopted another aspect of her theory. The court ruled that actions "sufficiently severe or pervasive" to create "a hostile or abusive work environment" violate the law even if unwelcome sexual demands are not linked to concrete employment benefits. The Court also agreed with MacKinnon that "'voluntariness' in the sense of consent" is not a defense to a sexual-harassment complaint. MacKinnon summed up the importance of *Vinson*: "What the decision means is that we made this law up from the beginning, and now we've won."

As shaped by MacKinnon, sexual-harassment law incorporates a key assumption of feminist jurisprudence: Women are at a fundamental disadvantage in a male-dominated society. In MacKinnon's words, "sexual harassment is the unwanted imposition of sexual requirements in the context of a relationship of unequal power." More generally, a practice is discriminatory if it "participates in the systemic social deprivation of one sex because of sex."

Systemic Inequality of Power

Since the inequality of power between men and women is systemic, a woman's consent is never completely free. Hence consent is not an acceptable defense against a charge of sexual harassment. The comments of Anita Hill's defenders reflected that understanding. In trying to explain why she did not file a complaint at the time of the alleged harassment, why she followed Clarence

Sexual Harassment

Thomas to the Equal Employment Opportunity Commission, and why she continued a friendly relationship with him for eight years, they cited a basic imbalance of power.

During the hearings, Sen. Arlen Specter (R-Pa.) asked Judge Susan Hoerchner, who testified that Hill told her about Thomas's harassment in the early '80s, whether Hoerchner had considered advising Hill to come forward. "No, Senator, I did not," she responded. "I believe that the tremendous inequity in power between them would have been dispositive."

Various commentators echoed the same theme. "The Judiciary Committee's dismissal of Anita Hill's story is about men not understanding what it is like not to have power," wrote Marie C. Wilson, executive director of the Ms. Foundation for Women, in *The New York Times*. "I'd like each man to think, think back to each and every sexual encounter and tell himself he wasn't playing power politics, he wasn't under the influence of a culture that says anything goes for men and women are the objects of the game."

Defining Sex as Rape

Similarly, MacKinnon argues that the reality of women's powerlessness within the patriarchy means that almost all of what passes for consensual heterosexual sex is actually rape. "Men see rape as intercourse; feminism observes that men make much intercourse rape," she writes. "Combine this with the similarity between the patterns, rhythms, roles and emotions, not to mention acts, which make up rape on the one hand and intercourse on the other. All this makes it difficult to sustain the customary distinctions between violence and sex. . . . If 'no' can be taken as 'yes,' how free can 'yes' be? . . . If sex is normally something men do to women, the issue is less whether there was force and more whether consent is a meaningful concept."

That view of women's subjugation within the patriarchy is crucial to the idea that a "hostile environment" is a form of sexual harassment. While the feminist jurisprudes might concede that a man could suffer sexual harassment in the narrower sense—for example, if his boss said, "Sleep with me, or you're fired"—they would insist that only a woman can be the victim of sexual harassment in the form of a hostile environment.

> *"Sexual-harassment law thus discards the idea of equal protection: Given the same alleged behavior, a woman will find it much easier to prove a claim than a man."*

In the 1990 case *Drinkwater v. Union Carbide Corp.*, the U.S. Court of Appeals for the Third Circuit explained why: "In the quid pro quo cases, sexual harassment claims are equally available to men and women, but non-quid pro quo hostile environment cases depend on the underlying theory that '[w]omen's sexuality largely defines women as

183

women in this society, so violations of it are abuses of women as women.'. . .
The theory posits that there is a sexual power asymmetry between men and
women and that, because men's sexuality does not define men as men in this
society, a man's hostile environment claim, although theoretically possible, will
be much harder to plead and prove."

Sexual-harassment law thus discards the idea of equal protection: Given the
same alleged behavior, a woman will find it much easier to prove a claim than a
man. The "hostile environment" approach also does away with the notion of intent. It does not matter what the defendant intended to do, or even what he actually did. The crucial test is the "environment" his actions created—in other
words, the subjective reaction of the complainant.

But as former *Newsweek* editor William Broyles Jr. noted in a *New York
Times* op-ed piece, "What is offensive to one woman may be obnoxious, amusing, or even endearing to another. . . . Each woman makes her own law." Such a
standard sacrifices a basic principle of fairness: that proscribed behavior must
be defined clearly enough so that people know when they're breaking the law.
It establishes government not of laws but of women.

Given the generous parameters of sexual-harassment law, many women could
make a plausible claim. Indeed, by MacKinnon's estimate, "around eighty-five
percent of all women are, or have
been, sexually harassed in the work
force at some point." (In an October
CBS News/*The New York Times* poll,
40 percent of the female respondents
reported having suffered sexual harassment.) The feminist jurisprudes
reject any attempt to constrain the
definition of harassment with traditional standards of reasonableness, which
they say have a masculine bias.

> *"What is offensive to one
> woman may be obnoxious,
> amusing, or even endearing to
> another. . . . Each woman
> makes her own law."*

Accordingly, in 1991 the U.S. Court of Appeals for the Ninth Circuit threw
out the "reasonable person" standard for determining a victim's harm in favor
of a "reasonable woman" test. Judge Robert R. Beezer wrote: "We realize that
there is a broad range of viewpoints among women as a group, but we believe
that many women share common concerns which men do not necessarily
share. . . . Men, who are rarely victims of sexual assault, may view sexual conduct in a vacuum without a full appreciation of the social setting or the underlying threat of violence that a woman may perceive."

Actual Women

The reasonable woman should not be confused, however, with actual women.
In March 1991 a federal district court in Jacksonville, Florida, applying the rea-
sonable-woman standard, found a working environment at a shipyard abusive

because of nude pinups on the walls and frequent sexual remarks and jokes. Although the plaintiff complained of sexual harassment, other female employees did not. The hostile-environment approach means that harassment is defined by the reaction of the most sensitive woman, even if she is the only one who takes offense.

> *"Harassment is defined by the reaction of the most sensitive woman, even if she is the only one who takes offense."*

As both the Jacksonville and the Thomas cases suggest, the feminist jurisprudes see pornography as closely related to sexual harassment. Together with fellow feminist jurisprude Andrea Dworkin, MacKinnon hopes to take advantage of what she considers the law's growing willingness to see "a convergence of pornography and sexual harassment." They hope that the concept of sexual harassment will help achieve the long-standing feminist goal of banning pornography. . . .

Pornography and Sexual Harassment

Now MacKinnon and Dworkin are working on a new law that explicitly defines pornography as a form of sexual harassment. They hope that this version, since it employs a rationale for restricting speech that the Supreme Court has already accepted, will satisfy First Amendment concerns. They plan to offer the model ordinance to the city of Minneapolis and to any other interested municipalities.

In the campaign against pornography, as in the areas of sexual harassment, campus speech codes, rape law, and the battered-woman defense, the feminist jurisprudes are working within the system, modifying it to mitigate the evils of the patriarchy. But as their rhetoric suggests, their ultimate goal is far more ambitious. They do not want to tinker with the legal system; they want to overturn it.

"Law is a potent force in perpetuating patriarchy and controlling social and political organization," writes Syracuse University law professor Leslie Bender. "Our legal system rests on an ethnocentric, androcentric, racist, Christian, and class-based vision of reality and human nature, all of which makes it inherently flawed. It is a system that resolves problems through male inquiries formulated from distanced, abstract and a contextual vantage points, while feminism emphasizes relationships, context, and factual particulars for resolving human problems."

So women have to start over. But there's a problem. Reality itself, according to these theorists, has a sex bias that must be corrected. "Feminist analysis begins with the principle that objective reality is a myth," the University of New Mexico's Ann Scales writes. "It recognizes that patriarchal myths are projections of the male psyche."

By rejecting not merely particular standards, but the idea of standards, not

185

merely specific arguments, but the very method of argument, the feminist jurisprudes seem to have disarmed themselves in the battle against patriarchy. "All of our norms and standards have been male," writes Bender. "If we extract the male biases from our language, method, and structures, we will have nothing—no words, no concepts, no science, no methods, no law."

Consciousness Raising

If, as Bender claims, all is patriarchy, how can women hope to create an alternative? The answer, according to the feminist jurisprudes, is that women can access an alternative reality, *their* reality, through "consciousness raising" (a.k.a. "C-R"). C-R is a process, not unlike A.A. meetings or group therapy, in which women tell their stories to each other. In C-R, writes DePaul University law professor Morrison Torrey, experience becomes a legitimate source of knowledge." By creating this new knowledge, MacKinnon says, C-R "affirms that there both is and can be another reality for women." In light of that reality, women can build a new system: "C-R clears a space in the world within which women can begin to move."

There seems to be no room for men in that space. If there are two realities, one for each sex, how can men and women coexist under the same legal system—or in the same society, for that matter? What is just for men is not just (if that term can even be used) for women. Some radical feminists, including Dworkin, therefore conclude that the only solution is sexual segregation—two societies, two legal systems, two civilizations. MacKinnon does not address this issue directly, saying only that no answer can be found within the patriarchy.

But the implications are profound. For if men and women are so different that they cannot truly communicate with each other, cannot even live together without one sex oppressing the other, the project of feminist jurisprudence is doomed at the outset. Since the feminist jurisprudes cannot persuade men that their way is better, the struggle to end patriarchy is a pure power struggle—one that the feminists, according to their own premises, are destined to lose. The reason for change—that men are more powerful in the current system—is the reason why things will remain the same.

In truth, however, the success that the feminist jurisprudes have so far enjoyed is based on their ability to use the very patriarchal tools they

> *"[Women] do not want to tinker with the legal system; they want to overturn it."*

supposedly reject: legal concepts, moral reasoning, general principles, and so on. If they have been able to change the law, it's because they have convinced men like Judge Robert Beezer, Sen. Ted Kennedy, and even Clarence Thomas—who fought for stronger measures against sexual harassment as chairman of the EEOC—that such changes make the law more just. Despite the supposedly unbridgeable gulf between men and women, the reformers have managed to communicate quite effectively.

To be sure, the feminist jurisprudes have weapons other than rational persuasion. By creating new sex crimes and imbuing them with the graveness of rape, they strike terror in the hearts of politicians, managers, academics, and anyone else who might oppose them. But they could not create those crimes without the collaboration of men as legislators, judges, and voters. And that collaboration belies all the talk of male/female, connected/separate, rights-based/care-based dichotomies. Like so many theorists who get involved in politics, the feminist jurisprudes seem to have abandoned their principles.

Legal Definitions of Sexual Harassment Threaten Free Speech

by *The New Republic*

About the author: The New Republic *is a weekly journal of opinion.*

For all its luridness, absurdity, and brutality, the television trial of Clarence Thomas had at least one laudable side effect. It raised the public's awareness of sexual harassment in the workplace, and may even serve to discourage it in future. As senators not previously known for their concern about women fell over each other to show their sensitivity to the nuances of sexual harassment, men around the country wondered whether they might be guilty of inappropriate conduct themselves. But by also revealing the elasticity of the legal definition of sexual harassment, the hearings could have another effect as well. They could ultimately cause harassment charges to be taken less seriously. Because the legal definition includes any unwanted "verbal conduct" that contributes to an "intimidating, hostile, or offensive working environment," it may lead to an outpouring of charges based less upon legitimate claims of harm than upon an increasingly powerful impulse to censor speech merely because it is offensive.

A Hostile Environment

Invented in the 1970s by the feminist legal theorist Catharine MacKinnon, and endorsed in 1986 by the Supreme Court, the "hostile environment" test threatens to trivialize legitimate claims of sexual harassment by equating sexual assaults with pin-up calendars, and by diverting attention from genuine, harmful sex discrimination. It represents a radical new exception to the First Amendment axiom that speech cannot be punished just because it is offensive. Like restrictions on "hate speech," it punishes expression where it should punish harm. This would present a dilemma for civil libertarians if there weren't any other way to protect victims of real harassment. But there is.

The Civil Rights Act of 1964 says nothing about sexual harassment, and before the 1970s, courts dismissed the idea that offensive words—without physical, psychological, or economic harm—could add up to sex discrimination under Title VII. But in 1980, influenced by Professor MacKinnon's arguments, the Equal Employment Opportunity Commission adopted three tests for deciding whether "unwelcome verbal or physical conduct" violates the Civil Rights Act: first, is it "quid pro quo" behavior that makes submission to sex an implicit or explicit condition of advancement? Second, is it behavior that "unreasonably interferes with an individual's job performance"? And third, is it behavior that creates an "intimidating, hostile, or offensive working environment"?

Speech and Conduct

We have no problems with the first two tests. But the third one is another matter. It relies heavily on the ambiguous term "verbal conduct," obscuring the most important distinction in First Amendment doctrine, which insists that the lines between speech and conduct be drawn as precisely as possible. And in upholding the test, the Supreme Court never explained why unpleasant speech that *didn't* interfere with job performance could be regulated in any way. The ambiguous test then became unintelligible. Courts decided that legality of speech would depend, in retrospect, on whether a "reasonable woman" would have found that it created an "intimidating, hostile, or offensive" environment. This turns the First Amendment on its head. The Supreme Court has traditionally protected offensive speech because "one man's vulgarity is another man's lyric." Under the new rules, speech can be banned whenever one man's lyric becomes a reasonable woman's vulgarity. The fact that men and women often find different things funny (not to mention the fact that women themselves find different things funny) makes the "reasonable woman" standard even more perverse.

To prove the point, a federal appeals court found in January 1991 that even "well-intentioned compliments" from officemates can count as sexual harassment. An IRS [Internal Revenue Service] agent in San Mateo, California, asked a fellow agent out to lunch twice, and after she declined, he declared his love in a poignant note praising her "style and elan," but promising to leave her alone if she asked. She sued and—because the

> *"The Supreme Court never explained why unpleasant speech that* **didn't** *interfere with job performance could be regulated in any way."*

court found that a "reasonable woman" would have found the note unwelcome—won. Days later a Florida district judge ordered the owner of a shipyard to stop his male welders from displaying pin-up calendars and telling dirty jokes. His logic: "[B]anning sexist speech in the workplace does not censor such speech everywhere and for all time."

These cases are disturbing on two levels. First, they suggest that harassment claims tend to be trivial or imagined, when clearly most of them are not. It is impossible to wade through sexual harassment cases without being shocked by the sordidness—and the extent—of the abuse that many women experience at work. The scatology that runs throughout the opinions would make Long Dong Silver blush. But if men are enjoined by courts from writing unwanted love letters, they will find it much harder to take real harassment seriously.

> *"Under the new rules, speech can be banned whenever one man's lyric becomes a reasonable woman's vulgarity."*

Second, it's scary to suggest that the rights of expression (including the right to ask for dates) should be less protected at work than at home. Work is where most Americans spend most of their waking hours; they must be free to express themselves verbally without fear of prosecution. Professor MacKinnon is correct when she argues that the logic of the "hostile environment" exception cannot be limited to the workplace, which is why it should apply neither in the office nor outside of it.

A Limited Definition

The solution to this mess is a definition of sexual harassment that excludes verbal harassment that has no other effect on its recipient than to create an unpleasant working environment. Sexual harassment, as the ACLU [American Civil Liberties Union] argues, should be limited to expression that is directed at a specific employee and that "demonstrably hinders or completely prevents his or her continuing to function as an employee." This would refine the existing test for "unreasonable interference." Either version would cover legitimate claims. As a 1989 note in the *Yale Law Journal* points out, *all* women who have successfully sued their supervisors (not their co-workers) for creating a "hostile environment" have also suffered some tangible economic harm, such as being fired. Dropping the hostile environment standard wouldn't permit real harassment by co-workers either. Even though it rarely presents an economic threat, such assaults often interfere with job performance. The law against sexual harassment would be strengthened, not weakened.

Assume, for example, that Anita Hill's charges are true. She would not need a "hostile environment" test to make her case. She might have trouble proving "quid pro quo" harassment, which occurs, according to the EEOC, when submission to (or rejection of) sexual advances is used as the basis for employment decisions. She concedes that her refusal to date Mr. Thomas and to watch bestiality videos didn't stop her from being promoted on schedule. Ms. Hill could argue, however, that Mr. Thomas's advances "unreasonably interfered" with her job performance. She was sent to the hospital with nervous cramps, told her friends she had become depressed, and eventually left the EEOC because she felt unable to continue. The judge in her case would still have to make a difficult, subjective decision about how much the harassment had interfered with her job, and how much interference is "reasonable." But these are the kinds of murky decisions that judges make every day, and they are far more appropriate than decisions about what a reasonable woman would find offensive.

What would be excluded from the legal definition of sexual harassment if the "hostile environment" test were abandoned? Only sexual expression that is offensive but that has no detectable effect on job performance. That would include most pin-up calendars, most well-intentioned compliments, and even some gross remarks. But trivial complaints like these are unusual. Sexual harassment lawyers say that cases of verbal harassment where the woman cannot prove physical or psychological damage are rarely successful in court, even under the "hostile environment" test.

Abandoning the "hostile environment" test is in the best interest of feminists as well as civil libertarians. The only realistic way to narrow the gap between what reasonable women and men perceive as harassment is to persuade men that unwanted advances can hurt women in tangible ways. A definition of harassment that diverts attention from that question makes relief for women all the more remote.

Feminist Legal Definitions of Sexual Harassment Will Result in Injustice

by Nicholas Davidson

About the author: *Nicholas Davidson is the author of* The Failure of Feminism *and editor of* Gender Sanity: The Case Against Feminism.

When dealing with an issue as fraught with emotion and ideology as sexual harassment, it is worth beginning with the obvious. Sexual harassment is a feminist issue. Feminists have raised the issue, defined it, and pushed for the laws and regulations relative to it. Therefore, to understand the issue of sexual harassment, we must first understand the nature of feminism.

Again it is easiest to start with the obvious, the dictionary definition of feminism. According to Webster's New Unabridged Dictionary, feminism is "(a) the theory that women should have political, economic, and social rights equal to those of men; (b) the movement to win such rights for women." Feminism may be more, of course; but we can expect to find some considerable correspondence between this definition and the actual views of contemporary feminists.

Nature of Feminism

With this definition in mind, we can profitably approach a question that has increasingly preoccupied sophisticated feminists, and which can be called "the contradiction." As discussed at length by longtime feminist activist Ann Snitow in a recent article in *Dissent*, and by several feminist academics in two recent anthologies, *Theoretical Perspectives on Sexual Difference* and *Making a Difference: Psychology and the Construction of Gender*, the contradiction consists in this: on the one hand, feminists reject the concept of an inherent gendered human nature. Personality differences between human beings in general, and between men and women in particular, are held to be purely the result of social "conditioning." As Kate Millett wrote in *Sexual Politics*, the book that more than any other established the intellectual respectability of feminism, it is doubtful that there are "any significant inherent differences between male and female beyond the biogenital ones we already know. Conditioning runs in a circle of self-perpetuation and self-fulfilling prophecy." This viewpoint derives from the environmental determinism of modern social science, and of cultural anthropology in particular, which in turn can be traced to John Locke's assertion in the *Essay Concerning Human Understanding* that man is born as a "blank slate." The actual expression Locke used is "white paper." On this paper, society writes whatever it wishes, literally creating human nature. This viewpoint, as applied to the sexes, I propose to call "unisexism"—the belief that there are no inherent differences between the sexes, and that whatever differences exist are socially constructed.

To this viewpoint in the field of human nature corresponds another in the field of public policy: that laws and mores should draw no distinction between the sexes, since such distinctions are, in the final analysis, artificial and to draw such distinctions is to judge individuals unfairly on the basis of arbitrary characteristics. Unisexism is both a theory of human personality and a program for action.

Unisexism

Unisexism was the most conspicuous perspective advocated by the modern feminist movement in its initial phase in the late 1960s through the 1970s. Feminists who emphasize unisexism, such as Simone de Beauvoir and Betty Friedan, tend to see women as cut off from the sources of meaning in life, which are monopolized by men. Unisexists display a strong tendency to devalue the feminine and are vulnerable to the charge launched by the antifeminists of yore that they aspire to male imitation. In *The Feminine Mystique*, Friedan went so far as to assert that women, as they presently exist, are "inferior to men, dependent, passive, incapable of thought or decision."

Beginning in the late 1970s, however, awareness of another perspective within feminism began to dawn on sophisticated feminists. This new awareness was brought home to many of them by two books, Nancy Chodorow's *The Reproduction of Mothering* (1978) and, above all, Carol Gilligan's *In a Different Voice* (1982). While environmental determinism remained prominent in the works of these writers, especially in Chodorow's, another perspective was introduced alongside it. Chodorow and Gilligan argued that a male-dominated culture had historically undervalued women's distinct "voice," which constituted an ethic of care, nurturance, and "moral pragma-

"The dictionary definition of feminism overlies a more complex reality."

tism" opposed to the abstract, judgmental, and absolutist values they attributed to masculinity. While the emphasis of unisexists tended to be anti-feminine, here the emphasis tended to be anti-masculine and may be called "female chauvinism."

Female Chauvinism

To female chauvinism in the sphere of human behavior corresponds in turn a program for action in the political realm, what is sometimes condemned and sometimes praised as "special rights and privileges for women." With the ascendancy of the female chauvinist perspective in the 1980s, feminist organizations frequently shifted from egalitarian positions, such as no-fault divorce, to sponsoring laws specifically intended to benefit women, such as the automatic assignment of mother custody in divorce along with generous property division and alimony settlements.

Discussing the contradiction in *Theoretical Perspectives on Sexual Difference*, Alison Jaggar argues that "feminists should embrace both horns of this dilemma. . . . They should use the rhetoric of equality in situations where women's interests clearly are being damaged by their being treated either differently from or identically with men." The results of this embrace are visible in many areas of modern life. For instance, colleges for men have been sexually integrated, often forcibly, as in the Justice Department's current suit against the Virginia Military Institute, one of a handful of holdouts. Many all-female colleges, however, remain in existence, including Smith College, which alumna Betty Friedan has aptly described as "the fountainhead of feminism."

> *"Unisexism thus generates female chauvinism, despite the evident contradiction between these two points of view."*

Hence we see that the dictionary definition of feminism overlies a more complex reality. Feminism, it seems, is a dual point of view and, on the face of it, these points of view are incompatible. One lauds androgyny, which it tends to see in predominantly masculine terms; the other lauds femininity, rescued from the unisexist devaluation of the feminine, at the price of a devaluation of the masculine. As early as 1973, the antifeminist writer Arianna Stassinopoulos summarized this contradiction in *The Female Woman*. In the final analysis, she stated, feminists "cannot decide whether they want to become men or destroy them.". . .

Defining Feminism

The original definition, from which we started, described feminism as "the theory that women should have political, economic, and social rights equal to those of men." This theory presumes that women do not, in fact, have rights equal to men. Rather than dispute this theory, let us explore its implications. If women do not have rights equal to men, the inescapable conclusion, which no feminist will dispute, is that women are oppressed. Feminism thus must include the idea that women are oppressed. Without this idea, feminism would make no sense. However, it also becomes then necessary to explain how women are oppressed, or more specifically, who their oppressors are.

> *"The question of sexual harassment . . . is a feminist issue."*

From the perception that women are oppressed follows the perception that men are the oppressors. Society is held to be dominated by men for their selfish benefit. Note that the "oppressed" and the "oppressor" are moral categories— the oppressed are victims who have done nothing to deserve their fate, the oppressors are villains who have done nothing to deserve their privilege. The theory that women lack equal rights inexorably generates the proposition that women are oppressed and that men are oppressors, which, because oppression is a moral category, further implies that women are victims and men are villains. Reduced to simplest terms, this sets up the following equation: women good, men bad—hence women are better than men. Unisexism thus generates female chauvinism, despite the evident contradiction between these two points of view. Feminism is thus not either the belief that women are the same as men, nor the belief that women are different from men and superior to them, but it is both of these beliefs at once. In the final analysis, it is impossible to reject one of these beliefs and remain a feminist. Yet these two beliefs are mutually exclusive.

Consequently, feminism presents a stark choice: either reason is invalid—as most sophisticated feminists maintain in this "postmodernist" era—or the assumptions of feminism are in fundamental conflict with the nature of things. In the latter event, there is no other choice but to reject feminism and to go back to nature (conceived in an Aristotelian rather than a Rousseauan sense). Since the nature of polylogism, and its implications for feminism cannot be explored within the confines of this essay, let us proceed on the assumption that the reader does not find the rejection of reason plausible and is willing to posit a convergence between metaphysical consistency and reality.

What Is Sexual Harassment?

The question of sexual harassment, as has been noted, is a feminist issue. Three things are already known about sexual harassment: (1) as a feminist issue, it will be an attempt to obtain redress for women from men, with the former seen as victims and the latter as villains; (2) it will be mired in contradictory notions of women's nature; (3) these contradictions are unlikely to delegitimate the issue in the eyes of feminists. Consequently, non-feminists must attempt to evaluate the merits of the issue for themselves, apart from feminist claims.

195

Chapter 4

What, exactly, is "sexual harassment"? For feminists, who are defining the issue, it consists in pressure on a woman to submit to sex with a man, backed up by psychological, financial, or physical intimidation, short of actual rape. The presumption is that the man holds power with which he is able to coerce the woman, or which persuades him he is able to do so. The attempt to define and punish a crime of "sexual harassment," therefore, is part of a larger effort to fundamentally change the ethos of society, as that ethos is understood by feminists: to wrench power from the male oppressors and create an egalitarian society in which sexual difference will no longer be important and in which sexual hierarchy, in particular, will no longer exist.

Sexual harassment, it is generally accepted, may take place either as an isolated incident or in the context of an ongoing relationship, including a sexual relationship, and regardless of whether or not intercourse actually ensues. A standard scenario involves a male professor who proposes to a female student that she sleep with him in order to get a better grade. Similarly, a male supervisor who demands that a female employee sleep with him as a condition for continued employment is held to be engaging in an act of sexual harassment.

Many feminists, however, take this definition further and argue that "sexual harassment" consists in the creation of a climate of fear, intimidation, and hostility to women. A college student who utters in the classroom the notion that men are better at mathematics than women may be considered guilty of sexual harassment, and may, in fact, be subjected to sensitivity classes at a growing number of universities. (Incidentally, the empirical evidence is overwhelming that men are, on average, better at math than women. For example, the ratio of males to females who score over 700 on the math SAT is thirteen to one.)

Sex and Coercion

Similarly, many feminists also argue that the mere existence of a power differential between a man and a woman introduces an inescapable element of coercion into potential sexual relations. When a male executive proposes a date to a female subordinate, the relationship is inherently coercive. This is one of the principal reasons why the United States military now rigidly prohibits "fraternization," or dating, between personnel of different ranks and genders; the other reason being the effort to retain military hierarchy in the face of the leveling tendencies of Aphrodite.

> "The attempt to define and punish a crime of 'sexual harassment' . . . is part of a larger effort to fundamentally change the ethos of society."

Threat of punishment for sexual harassment constitutes a growing element in the lives of Americans. It is clear that the oft-predicted demise of feminism is chimerical and feminism continues to represent a major factor in the evolution

196

of society.

As the case of the military suggests, the sexual harassment issue represents in part a reaction to a real problem. With the two sexes cast together in close proximity for long periods of time, the possibilities for sexual contact, and hence for sexual conflict, are vastly multiplied compared to those that exist in a more traditional society. The need to fend off unwanted male advances may well be a greater problem for women today than it was in the past. The sexual revolution, with its rupturing of all traditional sexual taboos that once condemned all sexual relations save those between man and wife, has infinitely expanded the field of potential sexual partners for both sexes, rendering all women fair game.

In this sense, women's liberation has produced women's oppression—hence, in part, the turn in feminism from a unisexist emphasis to a female chauvinist one. For women to participate equally in society now seems to many feminists to require special rights and privileges. As feminist writer Sylvia Hewlett argues in *A Lesser Life*: "Women . . . need more than equality with men if they are to attain equal earning power." Ironically, this change is far from unwelcome to many traditionalists, heralding as it does a partial rollback of the sexual revolution. Yet the feminist account of sexual harassment contains some disquieting elements. For one thing, it easily shades into fanaticism, as numerous examples from college campuses indicate. For example, in 1989, a University of Toronto mathematics professor was convicted of "sexual harassment" for allegedly staring at a

> *"Threat of punishment for sexual harassment constitutes a growing element in the lives of Americans."*

part-time female student at the university pool. He was severely reprimanded and forced to undergo extended counseling.

This behavior, if it actually took place, is nothing more than Italian or French men do in the street every day. Such behavior may be rude or intrusive, although anyone who has lived in Italy or France knows that it is considered rude for a man not to notice a beautiful woman. As the Toronto incident illustrates, what feminists are looking for is not simply redress for genuinely objectionable behavior, but a fundamental change of the mores of our society. The issue of sexual harassment extends far beyond questions of law to questions of culture.

Feminists Harass Men

A second incident is even more informative of the nature of sexual harassment as understood by feminists. In the spring of 1988, Pete Schaub, a student at the University of Washington at Seattle, was expelled from the university's introductory Women's Studies class for asking questions that were skeptical of some aspects of feminism. Numerous students present have testified that Schaub's demeanor was consistently polite. "What was his crime?" asked one of them, Shirley Hamblin, in a letter to the university newspaper. "He asked questions. He challenged instructors to support their claims." Campus feminists took this expulsion as the signal to start a university-wide campaign, using

> *"Women's liberation has produced women's oppression."*

Schaub as their symbol. They repeatedly accused him in the local press of threatening them. When questioned by reporters about the nature of those threats, they were able to offer nothing more specific than that Schaub, a body-builder, was large and hostile. "If that is threatening," Schaub responded, "I've been threatened many times. I've seen many big people."

Campus feminists, assisted by Seattle feminist groups, proceeded to hold a series of demonstrations against Schaub, whose only crime remained that he had asked questions in class. Schaub showed up at one of the demonstrations to see what was going on. When he was recognized, the crowd encircled him and chanted over and over: "Stop sexual harassment!"

Just who is harassing who? Are alternative conceptions of sexual harassment possible? After all, on the face of it, Schaub was guilty only of being male and having expressed some reservations about feminism. (Despite the treatment he received, Schaub has continued to express support for feminism in general.) On the face it—at least by the liberalized definition of harassment as the creation of a hostile or intimidating climate relative to gender—was Schaub who was sexually harassed.

Being "The Other"

The nature of the course in which he was enrolled also raises some interesting questions. Several Seattle lesbian feminist activists were brought into the classroom as guest lecturers, where they informed the students about the lesbian lifestyle as an option they might want to consider. The course syllabus contained this assignment: "During the first half of the quarter you are required to take part in an experience of being 'The Other' and to write up a two-page, typewritten, double-spaced summary of your experience. . . . " This experience may fall into two categories:

1. The experience of being a minority in a non-white dominant group setting, i.e., being the only white in a group, the only male, only straight person, only English-speaking person, etc.

2. The experience of becoming "The Other," i.e., ride a Metro bus visibly reading a lesbian book, use a wheelchair for one day, etc.

Not surprisingly, another student project that was suggested in the syllabus was "to join or organize a demonstration.". . .

When the Pete Schaub affair became national news, the Washington State

Senate held an investigation, which resulted in a mild reprimand to the university. The course is still one of the most popular courses, the head of the women's studies program, Sue Ellen Jacobs, told me and there will be no changes in its substance.

This raises the possibility that there are forms of sexual harassment other than those conceived of by feminists. Indeed, it is hard to see how feminism's fundamental assumption, that women are oppressed, can fail to lead to male-bashing. Could one not reasonably conclude that feminist studies, by their very nature, constitute a form of sexual harassment?

Yet, two wrongs do not make a right and the question of male harassment of women remains. It would be idle to deny that this constitutes a problem for some women. The fanaticism and, frankly, cruelty that seem to come so easily to feminists intent on slaying the dragon of sexual harassment, though, suggest that a more nuanced approach may be called for—one that does not see women as impotent and inevitable victims, and men as omnipotent and inevitable villains. Nothing could be clearer, to somebody who has lived a little, than that disappointed female lovers sometimes make real trouble for the men who reject them. Endless phone calls, threats, and even violence are hardly unknown behaviors for either gender. The scenario of the movie *Fatal Attraction* has been played out, albeit typically at a much lower level of violence, between countless men and women since the dawn of history, and per-

> *"Men are probably more prone to attempt coercion for sex, and women for love."*

haps especially since the sexual revolution. It is true that there may be a sex difference here: men are probably more prone to attempt coercion for sex, and women for love. This merely corresponds to a fundamental difference in sexual strategy that has been heavily documented by sociobiologists; it is hard to see what difference this makes to the victim.

Oddly enough, virtually all feminists will accept the foregoing statement if it is cast in terms of unisexism. Thus if you say to a feminist that women are just as powerful and strong-willed as men, and that they cannot be expected to take rejection lying down, she will readily accept the statement, even though, if consistently applied, it demolishes the notion that only men engage in harassing behavior in the sexual arena.

Feminist Contradiction

Here we approach the contradictoriness of the feminist position with regard to sexual harassment. On the one hand, feminists have endlessly assured us, women are "strong," physically, mentally, and morally—just as tough as men, equally able to take part in military combat and to endure the torture that is often the fate of the prisoner of war, and not especially concerned with the likeli-

199

hood of rape at the hands of their captors. To assert that there are sex differences—which means to a feminist, when she is standing on her unisexist foot, to assert that men do some things better than women, although it would make equal sense to conclude that women do some things better than men—is perceived as profoundly insulting. On the other hand, if women are as tough as men, as easily able to stand up to abuse and resist pressure of all kinds, why do they need the protection of special "sexual harassment" laws? After all, could a woman not just say no?

Here we encounter the profound influence of socialism on feminist thinking. Feminists are prone to assume that a woman threatened with the loss of one job has little prospect of finding another. Employment is seen as a scarce commodity (whereas in a libertarian economy, labor itself is in short supply). This assumption of employment scarcity leads to the concept of a job as an entitlement, which in turn reclassifies the employer as a servant of the state. Gradually, the private sphere risks being subsumed within the public sphere. Not coincidentally, a standard leitmotif of sophisticated feminists is to criticize the very existence of the public/private dichotomy. Traditionalists may take heart, from a very long-range point of view, for the logical result of the annihilation of the private is a castification of society and the destruction of liberal institutions. The alternative would be to assume that individuals are substantially capable of taking care of themselves, and that it is futile and destructive to attempt to regulate the minutiae of human behavior through the crude instrument of law.

None of this is meant to imply that sexual harassment laws and regulations will do no good. Women will be treated with somewhat more respect; some overbearing men will be frightened into restraining their impulses; and from time to time a genuine victim will manage to obtain justice for a real slight. But the increased regulation of the minutiae of speech and behavior will far outweigh this limited benefit. The concept of sexual harassment has already begun to claim its victims. The looseness of the concept of sexual harassment, and the fact that its justifiable ambit has already been perverted beyond recognition, should be sufficient warning against its implementation.

Feminists, ever ready to play on male chivalry, which they elsewhere condemn, often ask: "How would you feel if your wife or daughter were sexually harassed by her superior?" We should remember to ask: "How would you feel if your husband or son were falsely accused of sexual harassment?"

Ultimately the feminist perspective must be rejected along with the destructive chimeras it generates, and we must go back to nature, where men and women, not unisexism and female chauvinism, circle each other like twin stars, in constant tension and mutual dependency. For that tension is the Dance of Life itself, and not an ideological ramble into the absurd.

Bibliography

Books

Ellen Bravo and
Ellen Cassedy

The 9 to 5 Guide to Combating Sexual Harassment. New York: Wiley, 1992.

Lois Copeland
and Leslie R. Wolfe

Violence Against Women as Bias Motivated Hate Crime: Defining the Issues. Washington, DC: Center for Women Policy Studies, 1991.

Billie Wright Dziech
and Linda Weiner

The Lecherous Professor: Sexual Harassment on Campus. Champaign: University of Illinois Press, 1992.

Catharine A. MacKinnon

Sexual Harassment of Working Women: A Case of Sex Discrimination. New Haven: Yale University Press, 1979.

Susan Gluck Mezey

In Pursuit of Equality, New York: St. Martin's Press, 1991.

Michele A. Paludi and
Richard B. Barickman

Academic and Workplace Sexual Harassment: A Resource Manual. Ithaca: State University of New York Press, 1992.

Michele Paludi, ed.

Working 9 to 5: Women, Men, Sex, and Power. Albany: State University of New York Press, 1991.

Timothy M. Phelps and
Helen Winternitz

Capital Games: Clarence Thomas, Anita Hill, and the Story of a Supreme Court Nomination. Westport, CT: Hyperion, 1992.

Barbara Kate Repa and
William Petrocelli

Sexual Harassment on the Job. Berkeley, CA: Nolo Press, 1992.

Amber Coverdale Sunrall
and Dena Taylor, eds.

Sexual Harassment: Women Speak Out. Freedom, CA: The Crossing Press, 1992.

Susan L. Webb

Step Forward: Sexual Harassment in the Workplace. New York: Mastermedia, 1991.

Periodicals

Angela Bonavoglia

"The Sacred Secret," *Ms.*, March/April 1992.

Jerry Buckley et al.

"Watershed? Not Quite," *U.S. News & World Report*, October 28, 1991.

Bibliography

Terry Eastland   "Anonymous Chickens," *The American Spectator*, December 1991.

Suzanne Fields   "Is It Really Harassment?" *Insight*, December 9, 1991. Available from 3600 New York Ave. NE, Washington, DC 20002.

Ted Gest and Amy Saltzman   "Harassment: Men on Trial," *U.S. News & World Report*, October 21, 1991.

Marcia Ann Gillespie   "We Speak in Tongues," *Ms.*, January/February 1992.

Bell Hooks   "A Feminist Challenge: Must We Call All Women Sister?" *Z Magazine*, February 1992.

David S. Jackson   "'I Just Don't Want to Go,'" *Time*, July 6, 1992.

Elizabeth Kolbert   "Sexual Harassment at Work Is Pervasive, Survey Suggests," *The New York Times*, October 11, 1991.

Richard B. McKenzie   "The Thomas/Hill Hearings: A New Legal Harassment," *The Freeman*, January 1992. Available from the Foundation for Economic Education, Irvington-on-Hudson, NY 10533.

Richard Marin   "It's Not Just a Woman Thing: Many Men Do Understand," *The Washington Post National Weekly Edition*, October 14-20, 1991.

Gretchen Morgenson   "Watch That Leer, Stifle That Joke," *Forbes*, May 15, 1989.

Naomi Munson   "Harassment Blues," *Commentary*, February 1992.

David Niven   "The Case of the Hidden Harassment," *Harvard Business Review*, March-April 1992.

Rochelle Sharp   "Capitol Hill's Worst Kept Secret: Sexual Harassment," *Ms.*, January/February 1992.

Jill Smolowe   "An Officer, Not a Gentleman," *Time*, July 13, 1992.

Susan Brooks Thistlewaite   "Sexual Harassment: To Protect, Empower," *Christianity and Crisis*, October 21, 1991. Available from 537 W. 121st St., New York, NY 10027.

Miranda Van Gelder   "High School Lowdown," *Ms.*, March/April 1992.

Rebecca Walker   "Becoming the Third Wave," *Ms.*, January/February 1992.

Organizations to Contact

The editors have compiled the following list of organizations that are concerned with the issues debated in this book. All have publications or information available for interested readers. For best results, allow as much time as possible for the organizations to respond. The descriptions below are derived from materials provided by the organizations. This list was compiled at the date of publication. Names, addresses, and phone numbers of organizations are subject to change.

Center for Women's Policy Studies
200 P St. NW, Suite 508
Washington, DC 20036
(202) 872-1770

The center studies policies affecting the social, legal, and economic status of women. It offers publications on sexual harassment, peer harassment, and campus rape, including a guide for women students who encounter harassment.

Department of Defense
Office of the Assistant Secretary of Defense for Public Affairs
Pentagon, Room 2E777
Washington, DC 20301-1400
(703) 697-5737

The office is responsible for presenting the official positions of the military on current issues, including sexual harassment. It maintains one officer responsible for information on women in the military and publishes a brochure that discusses sexual harassment in the military.

Equal Employment Opportunity Commission (EEOC)
1801 L St. NW
Washington, DC 20507
(202) 663-4900

The purpose of the EEOC is to eliminate discrimination in the workplace. To achieve this purpose, the commission investigates cases of alleged discrimination, including cases of sexual harassment; helps victims prosecute cases; and offers educational programs for employers and community organizations. The EEOC publishes a packet of information about sexual harassment.

Fund for the Feminist Majority
1600 Wilson Blvd., Suite 704
Arlington, VA 22209
(703) 522-2214

The organization researches methods that empower women. It maintains a hotline at (703) 522-2501 that provides information, referrals, and strategies for dealing with sexual harassment. The fund also publishes a report that includes an overview and critical analysis of sexual harassment laws and an examination of women's experiences of sexual harassment.

Index